Comedy in Action

*For **Sophia Schaffer Blistein** who knows
how, where, and when to laugh*

Elmer M. Blistein

Comedy

in

Action

Duke University Press

Durham, N. C.   1964

© 1964, Duke University Press

Second printing, 1971

L.C.C. card 64–22154

I.S.B.N. 0–8223–0017–6

Preface

Prefaces, acknowledgments—call them what you will—are occasionally considered disingenuous or bromidic. Recently, as a case in point, a highly respected periodical saw fit to publish a devastating parody of what its author considered a typical university-press-book acknowledgment. Yet the life is so short, the craft is so hard to learn, and so few of us are self-taught that acknowledgments are not only necessary but desirable, motivated not only by honesty but by gratitude.

A grant from the Faculty Research Fund of Brown University was most helpful. I am grateful to the staff of the Film Library of the Museum of Modern Art, particularly to Richard Griffith, Margareta Akermark, Eileen Bowser, the ever-helpful Jo-Ann Ordano, and that most knowledgeable of all projectionists, Arthur Steiger. Beaumont Newhall and James Card quietly and efficiently made available to me the tremendous resources of George Eastman House in Rochester, New York. David A. Jonah and his staff at the John Hay Library of Brown University invariably and cheerfully produced whatever book or article I sought. For advice, suggestions, encouragement, and stimulation, I am indebted to Jess B. Bessinger, Hyatt H. Waggoner, Richard L. Grossman, and all the students who saw fit to take a course entitled "Comedy and Laughter" with me.

A person should never acknowledge indebtedness to his family for two very good reasons: his acknowledgment would inevitably be inadequate, and the individual members may at some time seek an impossible-to-produce *quid pro quo*.

E. M. B.

Brown University
Providence, Rhode Island
February, 1964

Contents

Introduction

xi

The drive for respectability: an aspect of the comic character

3

The object of scorn: an aspect of the comic antagonist

21

Cruelty and comedy (I): "You beat your pate, and fancy wit will come."

42

Cruelty and comedy (II): "When you say that, frown!"

66

Love, sex, and comedy

77

We the people are not amused

111

Bibliography

131

Index

140

*Finish the tragedy! No. I have finally understood. Certainly
everything is ugly, everything is sad, and afterwards we know
it. But the soul must be purged by laughter. The only virile
attitude to take in the face of the human condition is to laugh
at it. And that is comedy.*

—JEAN ANOUILH, *La Petite Molière*

Introduction

At the conclusion of Plato's *Symposium*, that convivial, intellectual treatise on love, the convivial finally overcomes the
intellectual because, we are told, someone had neglected to
close the door. We can accept Plato's reason, even though we
may be beset by doubt, because Socrates, alone of the company, remains in character:

Agathon arose in order that he might take his place on the
couch by Socrates, when suddenly a band of revellers entered, and

spoiled the order of the banquet. Someone who was going out having left the door open, they had found their way in, and made themselves at home; great confusion ensued, and everyone was compelled to drink large quantities of wine. Aristodemus said that Eriximachus, Phaedrus, and others went away—he himself fell asleep, and as the nights were long took a good rest: he was awakened towards daybreak by a crowing of cocks, and when he awoke, the others were either asleep, or had gone away; there remained only Socrates, Aristophanes, and Agathon, who were drinking out of a large goblet which they passed around, and Socrates was discoursing to them. Aristodemus was only half awake, and he did not hear the beginning of the discourse; the chief thing which he remembered was Socrates compelling the other two to acknowledge that the genius of comedy was the same with that of tragedy, and that the true artist in tragedy was an artist in comedy also. To this they were constrained to assent, being drowsy, and not quite following the argument.

We can sympathize with Aristophanes and Agathon. Drowsy or alert, we too are often "constrained to assent" when the theorists of tragedy tell us that tragedy and comedy are the same thing, that they do not need to discuss comedy when they have already discussed tragedy. They overpower us with the convincing respectability of an ablative absolute. "*Mutatis mutandis,*" they say condescendingly, "what is true of tragedy is also true of comedy." And off they go to contemplate the eternal verities, not bothering, as George Gordon remarks, to tell us what are the things that ought to be changed. Aristotle is guilty, Coleridge is guilty, Lamb is guilty, and Bradley is guilty. When gold rusts, what can you expect from iron?

If the critics would stop with their erroneous but innocuous statement about the similarity of comedy and tragedy, we should have no complaint. After all, they are not required to develop theories of comedy, or to meditate on the sources of or the reactions to comedy; they are not even required to like comedy. But most critics not only dislike but actively distrust that which they are unable to understand. I do not know whether Plato understood comedy—I feel he did not, but I cannot prove it—but he certainly disliked and distrusted both comedy and laughter:

> Our guardians ought not to be overmuch given to laughter. Violent laughter tends to provoke an equally violent reaction. We must not allow poets to describe men of worth being overcome by it; still less should Homer speak of the gods giving way to "unquenchable laughter" at the sight of Hephaestus "bustling from room to room." That will be against your principles.

His distrust seems to be born of an uneasiness in the presence of comedy, a fear of the effect that comedy can have on an audience, even though he realized, reluctantly, that the whole man should know about comedy:

> For serious things cannot be understood without laughable things, nor opposites at all without opposites, if a man is really to have intelligence of either; but he cannot carry out both in action, if he is to have any degree of virtue. And for this very reason he should learn them both, in order that he may not in ignorance do or say anything that is ridiculous and out of place—he should command slaves and hired strangers to imitate such things, but he should never take any serious interest in them himself.

The principle enunciated here may be accurately, if inelegantly, summed up, "Hang your clothes on a hickory limb, but don't go near the water."

Plato is not alone in regarding comedy as an entertaining but not quite respectable member of the literary family. Aristotle admits, somewhat apologetically, that comedy exists; Matthew Arnold's attitude toward comedy is made explicit when he relegates Chaucer to the Limbo of those who lack "high seriousness"; Chaucer himself demonstrates a certain uneasiness about his comic creations when he seeks spiritual respectability in his Retraction; even so great a master of the comic art as Molière wistfully remarks that making good people laugh is a strange undertaking. For frequently this apologetic, almost condemnatory, attitude toward comedy has been fostered by those best in a position to attack it, the practitioners of comedy. The comedians, actors and writers alike, have frequently taken a half-defensive, half-apologetic tone toward their art: the comic writer knows that his work is important, but he feels that he must write a tragedy to insure his fame; the clown wants to play Hamlet.

Such an attitude is, to a certain extent, understandable. After all, we all feel the necessity for variety and change in our lives, and we should not condemn that need in others. The need for change may be understood, but the apology for art may not be. There is, without doubt, a place for "high seriousness," a place for the tragic; but, since most of us live in the happy middle ground of life, neither too wise nor too stupid, neither too good nor too bad, neither unblemished saint nor sinner of deepest dye, there is definitely a place in our lives—and without apology—for the comic and comedy.

The critics and philosophers, the comedians and the comic writers, are not the only ones to blame for the offhand dismissal of comedy from the company of the learned, the virtuous, the respectable. All of us, readers, viewers, raconteurs, have to bear part of the blame. Most people do not believe that time spent on tragedy is wasted; they feel that eternal truths will come from such study. They may be right, but eternal truths can come from a study of comedy too. There is a further obstacle to a close study of comedy. If people do not like comedy, they may feel that to study it is to waste time; if they do like comedy they may believe that close analysis of comedy's effects is almost sacrilegious, that nothing kills a laugh more quickly than explaining a joke. While there may be some merit in such a belief, the logical conclusion to the hypothesis is that the more ignorant we are, the more we can laugh; the less we understand something, the louder we can laugh at it. Such a conclusion is untenable. Because it is untenable classical and medieval critics—some of them—sought to explain laughter and comedy on rhetorical grounds. In the past century critics have tried to explain comedy and laughter on sociological, psychological, philosophical, and anthropological grounds. Certainly Meredith, Freud, Bergson, and Cornford have much of value to offer all those interested in comedy and the comic, and certainly any attempt at a synthesis must include the medieval rhetoricians and the classical moralists, but the grave danger of working from the theorists is that the synthesis would tend to become synthetic, and genuine insight be perverted into *ersatz* cataloguing.

Therefore, there is no attempt here to write a history of comic theory. Neither is there any attempt to avoid mentioning the theorists of the past in an effort to appear autodidactic. It will be evident to anyone who reads that I am tremendously indebted to the theorists of comedy, ancient, modern, and contemporary. I did not, however, get interested in comedy because of the theorists; I became interested in the theorists because I was interested in comedy and laughter. It was not enough to laugh at something that was amusing. I wanted to know why I was laughing, why this was amusing, why that left me cold. Occasionally, I found the theorists very helpful as I attempted to soothe the annoying cerebral itch; at other times they were no help at all. I soon discovered that there was no universal theory of laughter. Aristotle would help in one place, Hobbes in another, Freud in still another, but no theorist or theory was universally applicable.

So there is one more caveat that I must issue: this book does not pretend to be a universal theory of comedy. A good working title for it might be "Some Notes toward a Definition of Comedy," or "Some Approaches to Comedy," or even "An Essay [using that word in its original sense] on Laughter and the Comic." But all of these and the title the book now bears are merely substitutes, and poor ones at that, for what, if I were permitted eighteenth-century style, I should like to entitle this book: "A Modest Inquiry into the Nature of the

Comic and the Laughable, with Some Animadversions on the Pretensions of the Comic Theorists, and Some Appreciation for the Creators and Actors of Comedy." Such a title would not be brief, but it would dispense with the necessity for a table of contents. In addition, it would be an adequate description of the book.

Comedy in Action

The world is a comedy to those that think, a tragedy to those who feel.
                    —HORACE WALPOLE, *Letter to Sir Horace Mann*

The drive for respectability: an aspect of the comic character

The respectable man is a serious man; the important man is a serious man. At the councils of the wise, only the serious are admitted. All these things we are told and told so often that they must be true. Yet, if they are true, how do we account for the flash of insight, the clear-eyed vision of the truth that comedy and the comedian so often provide? The critics of comedy have frequently pointed out that comedy is intellectual, tragedy emotional, as if it were possible to separate feeling from thought, the heart from the mind. But perhaps the comedian is kept from the councils of the wise just because of these clear-eyed visions of the truth. To most men, the truth is painful, particularly when they have made a mistake. Comedy has the unfortunate knack of seeing mistakes through masses of verbiage, storms of emotion, and clouds of rhetoric. The Fool in *King Lear* has taxed the old king with some home truths, and has been warned that the whip awaits him if he keeps on. His answer is perceptive, true, and couched in most homely terms: "Truth's a dog must to kennel; he must be whipp'd out, when Lady the brach may stand by th' fire and stink." The truth and the comedian are frequently tactless.

In an effort to account for the comedian's ability to see to the heart of the matter when many of the wise and serious so often fail, many critics and commentators have noted the salient fact that comedians tend to be, in their private lives, quiet, retiring, even morose. By so doing, the critics can be happy since they have maintained their formidable equations: seriousness equals respectability; seriousness equals importance. They not only provide the equations, but also provide the proof. The proof, strangely enough, takes the form of an anecdote about a clown. The story has been told about Grimaldi, about Rich, about Chaplin, about Will Kemp, about, I suspect, every great comedian. William Makepeace Thackeray, writing on Swift in his *English Humourists of the Eighteenth Century*, tells the story more economically and more universally than most:

> Harlequin without his mask is known to present a very sober countenance, and was himself, the story goes, the melancholy patient whom the Doctor advised to go and see Harlequin—a man full of cares and perplexities like the rest of us, whose Self must always be serious to him, under whatever mask or disguise, or uniform he presents to the public.

Even if this poignantly ironic anecdote is omitted, some other mention is generally made, in order to prove the equations, about the two faces, one private, one public, of the comedian. Gene Fowler, writing on Jimmy Durante in *Schnozzola,* and obviously writing before the first successful lunar probe, waxes mystical as he presents his proof: "The public knew nothing of Jimmy Durante's burdens. Laughing strangers care little about the private woes of their clowns. Who has looked upon the other side of the moon?"

The critics, the commentators, the theorists have frequently described, then, what may be called the Pagliacci Syndrome. The comedian is represented as a Janus-like character, wearing the mask of comedy on his obverse, the mask of tragedy on his reverse. But despite the descriptions, the equations, the syndrome, the proof, we are not happy. Too many obstacles have been placed in the path of true comedy, of joyous laughter. But haven't we made a mistake? Haven't we depended too much on the theorists, on the commentators, on the critics? What does comedy itself have to say?

So we turn from the theorists to comedy itself, and particularly dramatic comedy. When we think of dramatic comedy, the great comic characters come to mind, and they bring with them an obstacle which we anticipated but which optimism seemed to preclude: the obstacle, unfortunately, of conscience, of what the other fellow thinks, of propriety, of respectability. Seriousness, not laughter, has been traditionally equated with dignity; dignity is the *sine qua non* of propriety; and we all yearn and strive for propriety. Our equations are still with us. Not all comic characters worry about propriety, to be sure, but those who do not are generally the characters we laugh at rather than with, the characters whose discomfiture delights us, the characters who are, in short, the comic villains or the comic antagonists. With them I am not at this moment concerned. I am concerned with some of our favorite comic characters in the drama who are not completely immune to this infection of propriety. Even Falstaff, that "trunk of humours," that "huge bombard of sack," briefly contemplates reform and propriety: "If I do grow great, I'll grow less; for I'll purge, and leave sack, and live cleanly, as a nobleman should do." But, perhaps fortunately, the pun on *great* and *less* is too tempting to leave alone, and the prospect of reform is, in fact, dispensed with before the possibility of reform is completely voiced. But the prospect was, albeit briefly, in mind.

Sir Toby Belch and Feste bravely taunt the complaining respectable who take a dim view of tinkers' gabble and coziers' catches late at night, but cakes and ale and even hot ginger inevitably seem to lead to a broken head, a bedside but respectable marriage, and Sir Toby's most terrible out-of-character line, "I hate a drunken rogue." Feste manages to remain in character—he even insists on his part in the plot: "I was one, sir, in this interlude; one Sir Thopas, sir. But that's all one." But Feste is comic only on the periphery of his being. In the center he is more suited to the concert stage than to the burlesque house; he is more singer than fool, more philosopher than clown, more dignified in motley than most men are in morning coats and striped trousers.

Touchstone, that rarest of fools, presses in "amongst the rest of the country copulatives" to achieve the propriety and respectability of marriage. He plans to make a lady out of his Audrey, "A poor virgin, sir, an ill-favour'd thing, sir, but mine own." He doesn't even wait until he is married to begin the lessons, "(bear your body more seeming, Audrey)" for the courtier's spirit is strong within him: "I have trod a measure; I have flatt'red a lady; I have been politic with my friend, smooth with mine enemy; I have undone three tailors; I have had four quarrels, and like to have fought one." Pygmalions never learn to keep their Galateas safe in stone or safe in the forest of Arden or even safe at 27A Wimpole Street; once stone has been exchanged for living flesh, and the forest for a Duke's court, and Wimpole Street for a splendid formal reception, the creator becomes the victim, if not the butt, of his creation.

Alfred Doolittle, the magnificent dustman, knows so clearly that the difference between five pounds and ten pounds is the difference between fun and respectability: "Ten pounds is a lot of money: it makes a man feel prudent like; and then good-bye to happiness." Firm in his determination to remain one of the undeserving poor, he successfully withstands the blandishments of the extra five pounds: "You give me what I ask you, Governor: not a penny more, and not a penny less." A man of such moral courage will not leave us, we feel sure; a man of such conviction will remain faithful to his station, faithful to his trust; a man of this stature will have no contemptible middle-class notions of respectability and propriety. The end of the play, however, finds him the tragic victim of an annuity of 4,000 pounds, clothes of proper cut, and the respectability of an impending marriage. Middle-class morality, a patently absurd synonym for propriety, has done him in. I call him a tragic victim because, like Othello, he is so aware of what has happened to him:

Thats the tragedy of it maam. It's easy to say chuck it; but I havnt the nerve. Which of us has? We're all intimidated. Intimidated, maam; that's what we are. What is there for me if I chuck it but the workhouse in my old age? I have to dye my hair already to keep my job as a dustman. If I was one of the deserving poor, and had put by a bit, I could chuck it; but then why should I, acause the deserving poor might as well be millionaires for all the happiness they ever has. They dont know what happiness is. . . . Intimidated: thats what I am. Broke. Bought up. Happier men than me will call for my dust, and touch me for their tip; and I'll look on helpless, and envy them.

A slight touch of his former carefree character is evidenced a moment later when, in reply to Higgins' statement, "Doolittle: either youre an honest man or a rogue," he replies (the stage direction says, "tolerantly"), "A little of both, Henry, like the rest of us: a little of both." But respectability and propriety are not to be denied. As he leaves Mrs. Higgins' flat to go to the church where his spirit-broken wife-to-be awaits, he may be heard musing, "Bridegroom. What a word! It makes a man realize his position, somehow."

So money or marriage or sometimes a combination of the two tends to make great comic characters achieve respectability. Unfortunately, respectability seems to be—at least to these people—a synonym for seriousness. But money and marriage, alone or in combination, are not the only sobering influences. I am not making an attempt at alliteration here, but surely music should be added to money and marriage. A hint in this direction was dropped earlier when the honey-voiced Feste was claimed as a philosophically serious character rather than a clown. Surely, too, the example of Harpo in the Marx Brothers' movies is another case in point. The ineffable Harpo exploits to the fullest most of the resources of comedy that do not require speech. His horn, his genius for pantomime, and the well stocked pockets of his great coat even enable him to create visual puns and visual wit. This zany is, in turn, buffoon, roué, pantomimist, defender of the oppressed, oppressor of the powerful, chaser, and chased. Then, suddenly, a change occurs: just as comic relief is considered by many to be essential to tragedy, so the Marx Brothers seem to feel that serious relief is necessary to comedy. That's when Harpo makes a serious appearance. It is not always prepared for, to be sure, but it is always present. Sometime, generally at the height of the foolishness, a harp appears—*materializes* would be a better word. At least once—this in A *Day at the Races*—and possibly one other time, the harp is a remnant of a torn-apart concert grand. At that moment a change comes over Harpo: his face mirrors delight; lechery disappears from his eyes; deviltry disappears; his features soften and his mood changes. His onslaught (no other word seems appropriate) on the harp may be terrifying and unorthodox, but the result is startling. Caught in a snare of his own contriving, he is oblivious to the world. He becomes a lonely, romantic, almost tragic figure. Music has had this effect on him, as it has had on other men, and women too. It would almost seem that the effects of money and marriage are slowly deleterious to the comic character, while music is startlingly swift in its sobering effect.

Not perhaps so swift as music, but definitely rapid in its effect on the comic character is important position in life. Even Falstaff briefly considered reform when the prospect of high station was before him. But perhaps it would be better to take another character, not necessarily a comic one, to see the effect of exalted position on him. Prince Hal, for example, with the responsibility of Shrewsbury upon him is a far cry from the cruelly comic baiter of Francis, the tavern boy, a far cry from the vicious prankster of Gadshill. At Shrewsbury he has no time for laughter. He must fight, and to fight he needs a weapon. When Falstaff's "pistol" turns out to be a bottle of sack, the borrowing Prince has time only for the bitter line, "What, is it a time to jest and dally now?" before he is off to perform the duties that responsibility and position demand of him. We are not surprised at the Prince's reformation. Indeed, we are not even sure that a reformation was necessary despite the cynical comments of Hotspur, despite Henry's sorrowful laments about his prodigal son. After all, we have heard his soliloquy at the end of the play's second scene; we have been adequately informed that the "vile politician, Boling-broke" has a crafty politician son. The critics may tell us that Hal's soliloquy is an offense against dramatic propriety, and perhaps it is, but it makes explicit what men of action and affairs have always known: there is a time for a holiday humor, and a time for responsibility:

> If all the year were playing holidays,
> To sport would be as tedious as to work;
> But when they seldom come, they wish'd-for come,
> And nothing pleaseth but rare accidents.

Hal is not, of course, a comic character even though his comic scenes outnumber his serious scenes and the lines in his comic scenes far outnumber the lines in his serious scenes. He is, in effect if not in conception, a character who is his own foil:

> So, when this loose behaviour I throw off
> And pay the debt I never promised,
> By so much shall I falsify men's hopes;
> And like bright metal on a sullen ground,
> My reformation, glitt'ring o'er my fault,
> Shall show more goodly and attract more eyes
> Than that which hath no foil to set it off.
> I'll so offend, to make offence a skill,
> Redeeming time when men think least I will.

If we take his remarks literally, we are forced to the conclusion that his characteristics really do not change no matter how much his character seems to develop and mature and mellow. In this sense we may say that the same spirit motivates his treatment of Francis in *1 Henry IV* and Michael Williams in *Henry V*. In the former, he produces and stages the entire episode; in the latter he takes advantage of a circumstance which he has, in a larger sense, also produced and staged. Francis, though the son of a woman, may have fewer words than a parrot, but Michael Williams has the words and the wit to turn a promised beating into a glove full of crowns:

> WILLIAMS: All offences, my lord, come from the heart. Never came any from mine that might offend your majesty.
>
> KING: It was ourself thou didst abuse.
>
> WILLIAMS: Your majesty came not like yourself. You appear'd to me but as a common man; witness the night, your garments, your lowliness. And what your Highness suffer'd under that shape, I beseech you take it for your own fault, and not mine; for had you been as I took you for, I made no offence. Therefore I beseech your Highness pardon me.

KING: Here, uncle Exeter, fill this glove with crowns
       And give it to this fellow.

It must be passing fair to be a king, even if you do not ride in
triumph through Persepolis but merely wander through the
camp and note the qualities of people. Henry is in good company when he does so. Antony and Cleopatra, Vincentio, the
Duke of Venice, and Haroun-al-Raschid all found it salutary
to wander in disguise among the common people in order to
discover their thoughts, deeds, and emotions. Note well, however, that although Henry had appeared to Williams as a common man, he did not take the chance of receiving a box in
the ear according to the provisions of their agreement in the
night. After all, it would have been beneath his kingly
dignity to do so, just as it was beneath his princely dignity to
permit the sheriff to arrest his associates, or to permit the
Lord Chief Justice to jail Bardolph with impunity. In the
Williams case, Fluellen, the magnificent Welshman, is the
gull. By appearing as his own foil, Henry had provoked the
quarrel. Williams was rewarded with gold; Fluellen received
a box in the ear and tried to pay a shilling for the honor. But
Falstaff had been rejected and, indeed, was dead by this
time, and the desire for low comedy, so essential a part of
Henry's character, still required satisfaction.

But Hal, or Henry, as I mentioned earlier, is not a comic
character. He is serious, aware of his responsibilities, aware
of war and statecraft and rule. But he turns from the serious
not merely to observe but actually to engage in the comic. He
baits Francis, he robs Falstaff, he makes a butt of Fluellen, he
courts the princess all in an attitude of rich comedy. He takes,
despite Plato's dictum, a serious attitude toward the comic
and comedy. He is a participant, not merely an observer.
Therein lies his greatest strength or his greatest weakness: he
is a serious character who finds in the comic a reason for being
if not a reason for doing. Important position, both when he

anticipates it and when he actually possesses it, takes him from the realm of the comic, just as it has taken other, more genuinely comic characters. He enters the ordinary, everyday, comic realm in order to establish a contrast, or in order to render bearable the terrifying loneliness of kingship, of responsibility, of important position. Perhaps for the same reason Abraham Lincoln read Artemus Ward to his Cabinet.

While important position often tempers and even destroys the comic, when it lapses from position into mere officialdom it can, and frequently does, create the comic. Bergson, who insists on automatism as one source of the comic, says:

> But complete automatism is only reached in the official, for instance, who performs his duty like a mere machine, or again in the unconsciousness that marks an administrative regulation working with inexorable fatality, and setting itself up for a law of nature.

It is occasionally hard to decide where important position leaves off and officialdom begins. Most of the time, however, the decision is not hard to make. We may have doubts about Polonius, but we don't have any about Dogberry. Even Cassio provides one of the rare moments of comedy in *Othello* when in his drunknness he lapses into officialdom and insists on maintaining the official lines of demarcation between ranks:

> CASSIO: For mine own part—no offence to the general, nor any man of quality—I hope to be saved.
> IAGO: And so do I too, lieutenant.
> CASSIO: Ay, but by your leave, not before me; the lieutenant is to be saved before the ancient.

The prospect of salvation is not normally considered a humorous subject, but the rank-pulling of officialdom succeeds even in this rarefied atmosphere. Even the theologians who discuss the angelic hierarchies have never envisioned cloud-soft wings decorated with chevrons or other insignia of rank derived from a former, lower existence. Malvolio, too, probably belongs in the category of officialdom, but it is difficult to decide whether his position molded his character or his character made his position inevitable. In addition, he is a comic antagonist, not a sympathetic comic character.

It is the literality of the official mind that produces the comic effect. Bergson calls this literality *rigidity*, and equates it with his catch-all definition of the comic, "the mechanical encrusted on the living." There is something about officialdom that imposes on officials a fixed, rigid routine. This routine, in its place, has undoubted benefits. If the policeman follows a fixed order in trying all the doorknobs of the shops on his beat, he is probably more efficient than his colleague who tries doorknobs at random. If we, in our own homes, follow a fixed routine of locking one door and then the other, adjusting the thermostat, setting the clock, turning off lights before we get into bed, the chances are that we do not toss and turn with worry about an unlocked door, an unset clock, an overheated bedroom. In other words, there is a time when not comedy but efficiency is obtained when the mechanical is encrusted on the living. Comedy arises, however, when routine is imposed upon actions which do not require routine, or when the wrong kind of routine is established. Policemen *should* stop speeding drivers, and they *should* prevent loiterers from leaning against buildings, and undoubtedly there is a proper routine for performing both of these tasks. I feel sure that the proper routine does not include asking the speeding driver if he is going to a fire, does not include asking the loiterer leaning against the building if he is holding the building up. The officials' questions are, of course, rhetorical, expecting the answer, "No," and the comic character, aware of the rhetoric, can create comedy for the audience by using the official not as the creator of laughter but as the butt. At the beginning of the Marx Brothers' film, *A Night in Casablanca*, Harpo is discovered leaning against a building. A policeman comes along, asks the inevitable question, but receives the unexpected answer of a smiling, vigorous, affirmative nod of the head. Outraged at the unexpected answer (his routine, you see, has been disrupted) the policeman yanks Harpo away. The building, needless to say, collapses. Our laughter is directed at the policeman, not at Harpo. Not only has the building collapsed, but, if only for a moment, the entire rigid world of officialdom has collapsed. We are delighted, not because we do not have respect for officialdom but because the official has misused his officialdom and retribution has been swift. The Dogberries of this world do not have to mutilate language to produce comedy. They can become comic by making a routine out of their authority. That is the reason, I suppose, that many people buy, read, and enjoy the detective stories which have the gifted and imaginative amateur outsmarting the rigid, routine-minded officers from the local constabulary or even from Scotland Yard. Imagine Sherlock Holmes, Lord Peter Wimsey, or Sam Spade in a policeman's uniform! The policeman's lot is frequently not a happy one—to the policeman—but it is frequently a laugh-provoking one to the audience. *The Mikado*, perhaps even the *Pirates of Penzance* and *H.M.S. Pinafore* testify to the comic effect of the triumph over officialdom.

If, then, important position, responsibility, officialdom in general are sources of the comic, how is it possible that they can, along with money, marriage, and music, have a deleterious effect on the comic character and the comic spirit? There is no pat answer to the question, but there are approaches to an answer. The sociological and psychological approaches have much merit, and I intend to mention them later, but there is a purely literary approach that deserves some consideration here. I do not want to become involved in a discussion of the essential difference between an author's intention and a work's intention. I believe that such a difference exists, that an author can have one intention for an episode or a character and have the episode or character get away from him. I believe that Shylock in *The Merchant of Venice*, Mercutio in *Romeo and Juliet*, possibly Beatrice and Benedick in *Much Ado About Nothing* are cases in point. I don't believe that there is always or even frequently a difference between the author's and the work's intentions, but I do believe that the difference is occasionally there. Frequently, however, we see another phenomenon: the author seems to contrive a happy ending for a sympathetic comic character who does not, if we accept the characterization as given, deserve a happy ending. Yet he gets one and, as Dorothy Sayers points out, we have seen a miracle:

> Mr. Wilkins Micawber . . . is favoured by a miracle at the end of *David Copperfield*. He is a "good" character—that is to say, a character sympathetic to his author—and it is desired to reward him with a "happy ending." He is therefore packed off to Australia, where in defiance of his own nature and in defiance of the nature of Australian civic life in the last century, he becomes a prosperous magistrate. However consoling this solution of the Micawber problem, a little thought convinces us that any person less suitable to prosper in these conditions than Mr. Micawber can scarcely be imagined.

Miss Sayers may be slightly harsh on both Dickens and Micawber. Dickens may have been able to see (although I doubt it) that the same quality of mind that made Micawber improvident in the handling of his own affairs may have qualified him—better than most—to sit in judgment and handle the affairs of others. But we in America have an advantage that Miss Sayers did not have when she wrote her book: we have seen the case of a man who suffered financial failure in the handling of his own haberdashery business but who was successful—eminently so, according to some—in handling the affairs of a nation. Miss Sayers may have a valid point when she says that Micawber's rising to the state of a prosperous magistrate is a reward for services rendered. It is to my mind the wrong kind of reward, but it is the kind of reward that frequently is bestowed on a sympathetic comic character: he becomes respectable. Micawber becomes respectable financially because Dickens wanted to reward him; Alfred Doolittle becomes respectable matrimonially and financially because Shaw's perverted sense of morality or humor thought that this kind of reward was in order; W. C. Fields in *The Bank Dick* gets to be respectable financially and sartorially so that he can flaunt this respectability before those who had looked down upon him and to prove that a fast wit and a touch of larceny in the heart can work miracles; and Charlie Chaplin in *City Lights* gets the respectability of recognition for a thoroughly decent and selfless act which he had performed. Micawber and Doolittle were at the mercy of their authors, and so, to a minor extent, was W. C. Fields, but Chaplin made his decision alone. These decisions typify, I believe, the desire for respectability that gnaws at the mind of the creator of the comic character, author and actor alike.

But what are the reasons for this desire, this drive, that leads the comic character to seek respectability? One reason may be implicit in a story that Danny Kaye tells when he takes a break in the middle of his performance, waves the orchestra away, borrows a cigarette from someone in the audience, and relaxes in a confidential mood. The story concerns the first time that his daughter, then a child of five, saw him perform. He knew where in the audience she was seated and, although the spotlight obscured his vision, he shaded his eyes with his hand, located her, and asked if she were having a good time. Her answer was waveringly affirmative. A short time later he shaded his eyes once more, looked in her direction once more, asked the same question, and got the same answer, but this time the wavering voice had changed to a quavering voice. He was disturbed, but finished his act. At the end he went to his dressing room and, a short time later, she showed up, smiling bravely through tears. He naturally asked what was bothering her, and the answer, spoken through a fresh torrent of sobs, was, "I don't like people to laugh at my daddy." The story may be false, but I doubt it. Kaye's five-year-old daughter typifies the reaction of the average audience to comedy and laughter. Kaye may have been able to assure his daughter that if people didn't laugh at her daddy she wouldn't be wearing shoes, but again I doubt it. To his daughter, to the audience, indeed, to society as a whole, comedy and laughter are not respectable, not proper. It may have been in an effort to justify himself to his daughter, to his audiences, to society at large that Kaye took his world-wide trip on behalf of UNICEF. Certainly he used all of his comic devices to achieve acceptance and appreciation wherever he went. Certainly his artistry as a mimic endeared him to children and adults alike. Certainly, too, the results of his trip made him a man of serious stature, of respectable position, in short, a philanthropist who dispensed laughter instead of money. His trip and the television film that was its product showed that he was capable of high seriousness as well as low comedy.

But Kaye is not the only comedian who has had similar motivation and similar desires. The sympathetic comic character, the one we laugh with rather than at, is not a fool, a buffoon, or a clown. He is a thinking man, and he is able to think clearly enough to realize that an audience, even when it is holding its sides, feels charitable, kindly, even condescending when it approves a comedian's timing, delivery, or wit. He knows, too, that an audience stands in awe as it applauds a tragedian who has just finished revealing his soul. He may find it difficult to understand the audience's reaction. What has the tragedian got that he hasn't? He admits that comedy is occasionally raucous, unbuttoned, bedraggled; but just as frequently comedy is suave, smooth, urbane. Comedy, as well as tragedy, can wear a top hat or a crown, and the top hat doesn't necessarily have to be a target for an urchin's snowball. And even motley can possess dignity as the example of Feste shows us, and as the melancholy Jaques' line, "Motley is the only wear!" implies.

And what if comedy is raucous? Certainly the mad Lear's cries are raucous too. Certainly Oedipus is not suave or smooth or urbane as he stands with blood streaming from his empty eye sockets. Willy Loman may not wear motley, to be sure, but certainly his entire wardrobe does not consist of suits of solemn black. Pagliacci's motley certainly does not render him the less tragic. The comedian finds, therefore, that the obvious, superficial differences do not account for the audience's reaction to his art, and he then is forced to look not at himself as contrasted with the tragedian, but at the audience. And when he does look at the audience, looks deeply, I mean, he sees something that causes him to despair. The audience, attired in courtly robes, dinner jackets, or sack suits, is nonetheless essentially primitive in its reactions. All the outward manifestations of sophistication and civilization may be present, but there is a primeval urge in any theater audience that demands something more than intellectual stimulation, more than entertainment, more than comedy and laughter, if it is going to do something more than applaud. In order to stand in awe it requires a victim, a victim who is destroyed. That the comedian is unable to supply, for while the tragic character as well as the audience is essentially primitive, the comic character is essentially civil. Macbeth and Brutus Jones are primitive men who are unable to keep their imaginations in check. They must be destroyed, and the audience will stand in awe. Oedipus and Othello are primitive men who are unable to control their tempers. They must be destroyed, and the audience will stand in awe. Even Hamlet, the glass of fashion and the mold of form, permits the primitive instinct for revenge to overcome him. He is destroyed and the audience stands in awe. But Alfred Doolittle can adjust, even Lady Wishfort and Mrs. Malaprop are able to adjust, to a change in circumstances. Destruction is not for them because they are flexible. The spirit of compromise, the ability to see the human situation from more than one point of view, is the mark of the comic character, and that is another reason, I suppose, that the sympathetic comic character reflects his creator's desire for respectability. For the great, sympathetic comic character, despite Bergson's theory of rigidity, does not have a one-track mind, is not equipped with intellectual blinders. Some comic characters, the butts of our laughter, the ones we laugh at not with, are so equipped, but they and the comic villain in general are a subject for another chapter. For the sympathetic comic character, however, very often the opposite is true. Far from being equipped with intellectual blinders, he often develops an intellectual squint from his attempts to see both sides of every question. So, because he is civil and intellectual, he is unable to make himself a victim, a primitive victim, if you will, in an attempt to obtain from the audience the type of approbation that he desperately seeks. Since he is unable to emulate the primitive aspect of his audience, he identifies himself—almost in despair—with the sophisticated aspect, the veneer which the audience presents to the world. And when he does that, the clarity of vision which a comedian must possess tends to disappear. He then becomes civilized rather than civil; he becomes acceptable, even respectable, in the eyes of his audience, those whom it is his duty to satirize, to poke fun at, to attack. He identifies himself with his raw material. Once he makes this identification, much of his value is lost. He can no longer be objective in his satire, wit, humor, and comedy, and the result is very often distorted and ridiculous. When tempted to his previous satire and wit, the clichés of those he has joined rise readily to his mind. He feels

The drive for respectability / 19

that he is fouling his own nest, that he is a traitor to his class and kind. Imagine Andrew Joseph Volstead writing advertising copy for National Distillers.

Certainly, then, this drive for respectability on the part of the comic character merits our study if we are to give to comedy the same sensitive consideration that we have given to tragedy. And there is no reason why we should not. Fortunately, many creators and actors of sympathetic comic characters realize the dangers present in the drive for respectability, and they attempt to confine their yearnings to their private musings. They realize, too, that the stage and life need characters to laugh with as well as laugh at if the multi-faceted sanity and reasonableness that we call comedy is to survive. What we need now are twentieth-century audiences and critics who are sensitive enough and mature enough to accept comedy for what it is: a respectable art form that creates and fosters an attitude toward life that is vigorous, corrective, and penetrating. Then, perhaps, the creators and actors of sympathetic comic characters can dispense even with their potentially dangerous private musings. Then, perhaps, Hamlet will yearn to play the clown.

Hood an ass with reverend purple,
So you can hide his two ambitious ears,
And he shall pass for a cathedral doctor.
                    —Mosca, in *Volpone*

The object of scorn: an aspect of the comic antagonist

At one point in "The Importance of Being Earnest," Miss Prism, the absent minded nursemaid-governess, is describing a novel she had once written. In it, she says, "The good ended happily, and the bad unhappily. That is what Fiction means." When we watch or when we read dramatic comedy, Miss Prism's mildly ambiguous definition serves to comfort us when an obstacle is placed in the path of obviously true love, or when a sympathetic comic character is placed in a situation that is surrounded by difficulties. For when we consider dramatic comic characters, our thoughts most often run to the sympathetic comic characters, the ones we laugh with, rather than at. We think of Feste and Falstaff, Charlie Chaplin and W. C. Fields, the melodramatic Cyrano whose wit conceals a breaking heart, and Billie Dawn, the twentieth-century Magdalene. We think of them because all of these characters, to a greater or lesser extent, have aspirations towards a world that is outside the comic, the world of respectability. We think of them because, although we have only a sneaking awareness that they are better than we are, we have an open awareness that they are better than they appear to be, that their comicdom confines them to situations not good enough for them.

> gods what a terrible tragedy
> not to make good with the tragic
> gods what a heart breaking pathos
> to be always doomed to the comic

Few of the sympathetic comic characters would go so far as to echo "the wail of archy" from *archy and mehitabel*, but we frequently have the feeling that our favorite comic characters are "doomed to the comic." We will admit that there is no artistic justification for our feeling, but we will also assert that there are psychological and sociological justifications for such an attitude. That is why, despite a momentary twinge of regret, we feel pleased when the critics applaud the performance of such an inspired clown as Ed Wynn when he plays a serious role; that is why, despite slight overtones of condescension, we feel pleased when a comedian like Red Buttons wins an Academy Award for a serious role in *Sayonara*.

Although we think most often of the sympathetic comic characters, we should not confine our thinking to them. The extremely complex art form which is comedy has many levels, many avenues of approach, and the matter of character is but one. And even the matter of character is not exhausted by an exploration of the sympathetic comic character. We must keep in mind the comic butt, the comic antagonist, the comic villain. Call him what you will, he has one salient characteristic: he makes us laugh at him rather than with him. It would, however, be a fundamental mistake to assume that the comic antagonist is always a less complex person than the sympathetic comic character. Frequently such is the case, of course, and then the butt is merely a two-dimensional sheet of cardboard intended to be the target of a custard pie. Frequently, too, the butt merely has to slip on a banana peel or have a chair pulled out from behind him as he attempts to sit, and the audience, sublimating its latent sadism (as some psychologists tell us), or giving vent to its appreciation of the unexpected (as some critics of the Max Eastman school tell us), can be expected to burst forth with gales of laughter. Such characters, simple as they are, have provided enjoyment for generations of high brows and low brows. The middle brows may enjoy them and laugh at them too, but they feel, most often, insecure in their laughter, as if it were possible to lose intellectual caste by a display of emotional honesty.

But the comic butts of the slapstick school, enjoyable and laughable though they may be, do not concern us here. We are concerned with the comic butt who is more complex than the slapstick comedian, who is at times as subtle as the sympathetic comic character, who is worse than he first appears to be, who is at first in a situation too good for him. He is, in short, the reverse of the coin whose obverse is the sympathetic comic character. The drama knows characters of this nature. Such characters are Parolles in *All's Well That Ends Well*, Mr. Applegate in *Damn Yankees*, Harry Brock in *Born Yesterday*, Malvolio in *Twelfth Night*.

Parolles is more complex than the simple classical braggart soldier. The problem of Parolles is, fundamentally, the age-old one of the difference between appearance and reality. Parolles would have us believe that he is a warrior, a sophisticate, a wit, handy in battle, cosmopolitan in taste and language, dapper in dress. Many in his world believe the appearance, and some who are aware of the reality find it necessary and politic to stomach his absurdity. At his first appearance, Helena describes the conflict. She is talking of her love for Bertram when Parolles appears on the scene.

> Who comes here?
> One that goes with him. I love him for his sake;
> And yet I know him a notorious liar,
> Think him a great way fool, solely a coward.
> Yet these fix'd evils sit so fit in him
> That they take place when virtue's steely bones
> Look bleak i' th' cold wind. Withal, full oft we see
> Cold wisdom waiting on superfluous folly.

Helena is not the only one to see the reality. Old Lafew sees it also and readily smokes him out, but the rest, particularly the men, require time, much time. After all, his technique is not bad. Note him as he implies his bravery and experience in battle when some of the young nobles of France are setting off for the Italian wars. He and Bertram are to remain behind.

> Noble heroes, my sword and yours are kin. Good sparks and lustrous, a word, good metals: you shall find in the regiment of the Spinii one Captain Spurio, with his cicatrice, an emblem of war, here on his sinister cheek. It was this very sword entrench'd it. Say to him I live, and observe his reports for me.

Perhaps Captain Spurio is as illegitimate as the etymology of his name would imply (although he is mentioned once again in the play, it is significant that Parolles is the one who mentions him), and perhaps too, if there be such a person, the cicatrice on his left cheek came from a source other than the cowardly sword of Parolles, but who is to know? These nobles are young, relatively inexperienced in war and humanity, and Parolles is rapid with the convincing detail which cannot at the moment be questioned. Even Lafew thought him for two ordinaries to be a pretty wise fellow, and Lafew had age and experience on his side. How, then, can we blame the gullible youngsters?

So Helena unmasks him in Act I, and Lafew unmasks him in Act II, distilling the dram of reality from the vat of illusion:

> Go to, sir! You were beaten in Italy for picking a kernel out of a pomegranate. You are a vagabond, and no true traveller. You are more saucy with lords and honorable personages than the commission of your birth and virtue gives you heraldry. You are not worth another word, else I'd call you a knave. I leave you.

Instead of becoming infuriated at this attack, Parolles, as always, salvages the one drop of sweetness from the bitter cup: "Good, very good! It is so then. Good, very good! Let it be conceal'd awhile." The "goods" that he utters may be ironic, but the relief evidenced in the "Let it be conceal'd awhile" is genuine. Concealment of the reality and display of the appearance are ever his stock in trade. Lafew is unable to convince Bertram of Parolles' absurdity, but Bertram is a young and inexperienced man. Only older, experienced men can see through Parolles; but women of any age, Helena, Mariana, the Countess, find him transparent.

By the end of Act III, everyone save Bertram is aware of what he is. To convince Bertram of Parolles' cowardice and fraudulence, the French lords conceive a plot to expose him as a poltroon and a traitor. The plot is successful and Parolles, completely unmasked now, is left to his own devices, deserted by everyone, even Bertram:

> Yet am I thankful. If my heart were great,
> 'Twould burst at this. Captain I'll be no more;
> But I will eat, and drink, and sleep as soft
> As captain shall. Simply the thing I am
> Shall make me live. Who knows himself a braggart,
> Let him fear this; for it will come to pass
> That every braggart shall be found an ass.
> Rust, sword! cool, blushes! and, Parolles, live
> Safest in shame! Being fool'd, by fool'ry thrive!
> There's place and means for every man alive.

This speech alone, even if there were no other evidence, would enable us to see that Parolles is not the traditional, simple comic butt. Too often the comic butt is unable to understand anything, least of all himself. Parolles has no such problem. He has understood the reality of himself from the start, and this speech demonstrates conclusively his self-understanding. If he were in reality a brave man, this unmasking would never have happened. If he were possessed of a true sense of decency, such an unmasking would have destroyed him completely. He won't be a captain any more, but he'll enjoy the creature comforts as well as any captain. And his future is summed up in the key line of the speech, "Simply the thing I am shall make me live."

Parolles' hope succeeds. Lafew will take care of Parolles who, having been fooled, will thrive by fool'ry: "Sirrah, inquire further after me. I had talk of you last night. Though you are a fool and a knave, you shall eat." But Parolles must always remember what he is. Any attempted reversion to his former situation brings stern reminders:

> Good Tom Drum, lend me a handkercher. So,
> I thank thee. Wait on me home; I'll make sport with thee.
> Let thy curtsies alone! they are scurvy ones.

From artificial captain he has become a nobleman's genuine fool, and he does not mind. He is, in fact, grateful. The audience has laughed at him for pretending to be something he was not. Lafew henceforth will laugh with him for being what he is. The simple comic butt might have been ignored in the dénouement. This complex comic butt must be taken care of.

Mr. Applegate, from the George Abbott–Douglass Wallop musical comedy *Damn Yankees*, is in fast company when he is compared with the Shakespearean comic antagonists. Yet he belongs in such company if only because he manages to make the devil of the morality play into a flesh-and-blood character. If Parolles, as C. S. Lewis suggests, may be compared with Belial, Mr. Applegate definitely must be identified with Lucifer. Yet Mr. Applegate holds audience attention because he is not a type: he is an individual. He has no horns and no tail. I don't think his feet are cloven, but I must admit that after kicking a chair in a fit of temper, he does say, "Oh, my hoof!" He normally wears business suits, but in one scene he parades around in a flamboyant dressing gown. He always wears bright red socks. He has the disconcerting habit of plucking lighted cigarettes out of the air, and he explains his habit by the simple statement, "I'm handy with fire." He is able to answer the fatuous query of a couple of autograph hunters, "Are you anybody?" with the almost accurate, "Not a soul." He has the ability to be invisible when and to whom he desires, and passes off this remarkable ability with the debonair statement, "An amusing little stunt—it was all the rage in the Middle Ages." Perhaps most important of all, he appears "as if by magic" when Joe Boyd says, "I'd sell my soul for one long ball hitter." For, do not doubt it, Mr. Applegate is the devil in a twentieth-century sack suit and with twentieth-century problems. He has dispensed with some, but by no means all, of his medieval trappings. Although he first appears to the sound of "eerie music," he settles his deal with a hand shake (right *and* left hands). He thinks signing in blood is just a "phony stunt." He has more trouble with wives than with the Methodist Church, and he lets Joe Boyd, a twentieth-century real estate agent, talk him into an escape clause. His seductive agent, Lola, "a beautiful red-head, is just what the Devil ordered." But this succubus falls in love with her prospective victim, and Applegate had done so much for her too. After all, despite her youthful beauty, she is 172 years old, and had been "the ugliest woman in Providence, Rhode Island." Surely the medieval devil didn't have such troubles with his assistants.

But while he has dispensed with some of the medieval touches, and while he seems beset with twentieth-century problems, he still maintains a strong sense of history: "I am quite a famous character . . . I have historical significance too. In fact, I'm responsible for most of the history you can name." Then, when he is explaining to Lola her part in his present proceedings, he again uses historical simile:

APPLEGATE: Look, Lola, here's the tie-up. This is a mass torture deal like the thirty-years war. I've got thousands of Washington fans drooling under the illusion that the Senators are going to win the pennant.

LOLA: (*Enthusiastically*) Oh, Chief, that's awfully good. There'll be suicides, heart attacks and apoplexy. Just like the good old days.

His sense of personal history serves him in good stead when, despite all his precautions, his victim wants to exercise his option under the escape clause. He then reverts to the medieval devil: "Very well. An operation of this kind has to take place at the witching hour. So, at five minutes to midnight if you still want to go back, say the word." And the devil loses his victim, but he doesn't give up easily. His actions in the concluding scene are strangely reminiscent of those of Dr. Faustus in the concluding scene of Marlowe's play. He pleads: "It was in impulse and I regret it. But I'll make amends." He cajoles: "I'm not really a bad fellow, Joe—I'm just emotional." He rages in his frustration: "Listen to me, you wife-loving louse you belong to me. You crook, you thief, you two-timing false-faced swindler! You've robbed me, you've robbed me!" And these last lines are accompanied by his jumping up and down in rage and frustration as the curtain falls and the audience dissolves in laughter at the timeless devil, possessed of so much knowledge, frustrated by the potent power of a man's love for his wife.

Applegate is, then, an excellent example of the comic antagonist. He is more important to the plot of his play than Parolles is to his. Parolles merely seems to be domineering; Applegate is so. That is why our sympathy is with his victims, not with him. We want him to be cheated, and this play is very satisfying because he ends up cheating himself. When he makes his mistake and tries to erase the error, we are delighted that he is foiled. Martin Luther and Saint Thomas More have told us the devil is a proud spirit and cannot endure scorn, and our laughter is the more intense and the more pleased for that reason. For this devil, this Mr. Applegate, has been triply scorned: once by his minion who, contrary to all the laws of demonology, has been able to drug him and thus place him in an impossible predicament; once by his victim, who manages to elude his clutches; and finally by the audience, which enjoys his discomfiture. Luther and More may be right when they tell us that the devil cannot endure scorn, mockery, or laughter; C. S. Lewis is certainly right when he makes it clear in *The Screwtape Letters* that the devil can neither understand nor tolerate love.

Both Parolles and Mr. Applegate have a superficial smoothness, a veneer that is thin, to be sure, but that nevertheless exists. Harry Brock, the comic antagonist of Garson Kanin's play, *Born Yesterday*, has no hint of smoothness, no hint of softness about him. He has a certain rough, vulgar charm; but he has always done what he has wanted to do, despite any opposition, and he thinks that he always will. We have some idea of the kind of man he is even before his first appearance on the stage. In Washington for a brief visit, he has rented a two-hundred-and-thirty-five-dollar-a-day hotel suite. You don't have to be a communist to agree with the chambermaid who thinks that there ought to be a law against people who have that much money to spend on a hotel room—especially since she earns only eighteen dollars a week. We find out too, before his first appearance, the source of his income: "Ran a little junk yard into fifty million bucks, with no help from anyone or anything—except maybe World War II." When he first "stamps in," we discover that his name may be Brock but, according to the stage direction, "Gross is the word for him."

Despite all that we have heard about him, despite his crudeness and boorishness in his relationships with other people, we may feel that he is a diamond in the rough, a magnificent example of what a man can make of himself under our wonderful system of free enterprise. We don't feel that way long. His first business venture was a paper route, surely a good American beginning. But Brock got his paper route through force: "I bought a kid out with a swift kick in the keester." His next business venture was a junk yard. He got the junk yard through stealing:

BROCK: I'll tell you. I'm a kid with a paper route. I've got this little wagon. So on my way home nights, I come through the alleys pickin' up stuff. I'm not the only one. All the kids are doin' it. The only difference is, they keep it. Not me. I sell it. First thing you know, I'm makin' seven, eight bucks a week from that. Three bucks from the papers. So I figure right off which is the right racket. I'm just a kid, mind you, but I could see that. Pretty soon, the guy I'm sellin' to is handin' me anywheres from fifteen to twenty a week. So he offers me a job for ten. Dumb jerk. I'd be sellin' this guy his own stuff back half the time and he never knew.

PAUL: How do you mean?

BROCK: (*Relishing the memory*) Well in the night, see I'm under the fence and I drag it out and load up. In the mornin', I bring it in the front way and collect . . .

PAUL: So pretty soon you owned the whole yard.

BROCK: Damn right!

Starting out with force, he soon, as we have seen, moved to theft. Then he discovered the purchasing power of money is not limited to things. Money can be used to buy people: "I never met a man who didn't have his price." Money buys the bodies of some people, the minds of others, the souls of still others. So he buys Billie Dawn; then he buys a lawyer who, before meeting Brock, had the stamp of greatness on him; then he buys a United States senator. Why shouldn't he? After all, a senator to him (he speaks relatively, of course) is "A guy who makes a hundred and fifty bucks a week." Our sneaking admiration soon turns to dismay, then disgust. We see him browbeat everyone in sight: his cousin Eddy, barbers, chambermaids, bootblacks, hotel managers, the whole *dramatis personae*. We see him use physical force on his lawyer, on his cousin, on Billie, on Paul. We are not at all impressed with the fleeting glimpses we get of the sentimental, paternalistic side of his character. We feel that it proves nothing good about him that he has provided employment for the boy whom he beat up to obtain his paper route, for the man from whom he stole to get his first junk yard. These two people, and his treatment of them, may be a sign of a sentimental character; they are, more likely, symbols of his belief that money can do anything, even turn enemies into friends.

This gross character with his rude wit, his boorish charm, must be proved wrong. He must be shown that there are some things and some people that money cannot buy, some people whom force cannot frighten. The audience must be enabled to laugh at his downfall, partly to get the aggression out of its system, partly to demonstrate its approval at the victory of virtue over vice, partly to conceal, even from itself, its fears that the attitudes which Harry Brock represents are dominant in our culture. And Harry Brock does meet his downfall. His downfall is, perhaps, foreshadowed by his defeat in the gin rummy game which he plays with Billie, but there is a major difference. Billie wins at gin rummy through luck or skill. Perhaps, in such a game as gin rummy, there is very little of the latter, but she does not use force, she does not cheat, she does not lie or steal. When Billie and Paul finally do triumph over the force that is Harry Brock, their victory is tainted, only slightly, to be sure, but nevertheless tainted, by the fact that they had to use Harry's methods to beat Harry. We are not surprised at Billie's use of such methods. After all, she has been with Harry for a long time, and has picked up some of his habits. Indeed, she has for a small portion of almost every day managed to become the dominant figure in their relationship by the simple expedient of withholding from Harry something that Harry wants but that is hers to give. As I say, we are not too surprised at Billie because reformation does not obliterate memory, but we are surprised at Paul, the twentieth-century Galahad. For Paul makes common cause with Guinevere, and turns from a Galahad to a Launcelot. Pragmatically, the end may stand clear of the means in a case such as this, but morally, of course, it cannot. Paul and Billie steal papers which are most incriminating. If the contents of the papers are revealed, the bill which Harry wants Congress to pass will have no chance of passing. It does no good to argue that Billie, on paper, owns the incriminating documents at least as much as Harry does, for Paul has no stake in them at all. Then, after stealing the papers, they use them to blackmail Harry. Blackmail is not only an ugly word, it is an ugly deed. Harry will be kept in line, we do not doubt, but his attitudes have not changed a bit. Billie and Paul have departed, leaving Harry, Hedges his senator, and Devery his lawyer, in varying stages of gloom, despair, and chagrin:

BROCK: (*Trying hard to laugh off his disaster*) How do you like that? He coulda had a hundred grand—and she coulda had me. So they end up with nothin'. (*A pause*) Dumb chump.
HEDGES: Yes.
BROCK: Crazy broad.
HEDGES: Quite right.
DEVERY: (*Toasting, his glass held high*) To all the dumb chumps and all the crazy broads, past, present, and future—who thirst for knowledge—and search for truth—who fight for justice—and civilize each other—and make it so tough for sons-of-bitches like you (*to Hedges*) and you (*to Brock*) and me. (*He drinks*).

No, Harry Brock does not reform at the end, even when confronted with necessity. He remains the same because he does not really know the difference between good and evil, between virtue and vice. Reformation inevitably implies a realization that what you were was bad. Harry does not feel that way. He still feels that he and his methods were right. He made a miscalculation, that's all. Oh, yes, the miscalculation wouldn't have been so bad had the chump not been so dumb, the broad not so crazy. Harry remains the same, and the audience is delighted not only that he has been beaten, but that he has not reformed. After all, had he reformed, the audience out of some sense of spiritual generosity or of spiritual altruism might have felt compelled to join him in a rueful smile at his past, an understanding smile at his present, a hopeful smile at his future. As it is, the audience can laugh at him, not with him, laugh heartily that this yearner after power has been frustrated in his drive, that this bully has been bullied. Laugh at him too because he has been made forcibly, if momentarily, aware that some people cannot be bought, that some things are not for sale. And while the audience laughs, perhaps it may forget that though he was beaten at his own game, the victors had to use weapons that he too would have used. We sympathize with, we laugh with, Billie and Paul; we do not have to worship them. We laugh at Harry; and, because he has lost, we no longer have to detest him.

Malvolio in *Twelfth Night* merits our displeasure from the moment that he steps on the stage. His first words show that he is sadly deficient in humor. Feste, whom we have learned to admire, has been trying to joke himself back into the good graces of Olivia, and he has been successful. Olivia asks Malvolio if he doesn't think that Feste is improving. Malvolio's answer, condescending, superior, humorless, leads Olivia to describe Malvolio in terms which we applaud: "O, you are sick of self-love, Malvolio, and taste with a distemper'd appetite. To be generous, guiltless, and of free disposition, is to take those things for birdbolts that you deem cannon bullets."

Just as he dislikes humor, and this play is a comedy, so Malvolio dislikes music, and music is very important in *Twelfth Night*. Sir Toby, Sir Andrew, and Feste are engaged in drinking and singing and laughing. Like other men, in other times, they find pleasure in laughter, in song, in wine. Perhaps they have been a little noisy; perhaps they have had insufficient regard for those in the household who were trying to sleep; perhaps they should be quieted, even silenced, but the arrogant Malvolio uses the wrong methods. Instead of trying to joke the revelers out of their revelry, he adopts a holier-than-thou attitude which a more subtle man would have realized was calculated to enrage not subdue:

> My masters, are you mad? or what are you? Have you no wit, manners, nor honesty, but to gabble like tinkers at this time of night? Do ye make an alehouse of my lady's house, that ye squeak out your coziers' catches without any mitigation or remorse of voice? Is there no respect of place, persons, nor time in you?

Sir Toby at first tends to ignore Malvolio, merely suggesting that they were keeping time in their catches, and besides it might not be a bad idea if Malvolio went and hanged himself. But Malvolio continues his diatribe, and it is little wonder that Sir Toby now feels compelled to cut this pompous ass down to his rightful size: "Art any more than a steward? Dost thou think, because thou art virtuous, there shall be no more cakes and ale?" Certainly Sir Toby is probably drunk at the time, but drunk or sober he has sufficient clarity of vision to comprehend that a toady like Malvolio is not to be tolerated.

Words are not enough to destroy this time-pleaser, this affection'd ass, this fool who thinks himself "so cramm'd . . . with excellencies that it is his grounds of faith that all who look on him love him." Maria comes into the picture with a plot that will take excellent advantage of Malvolio's self-love. She will drop a letter in his path; the handwriting in the letter will convince Malvolio that it was written by Olivia; he will take the dictates of the letter to heart, and will act in accordance with them. Both his discovery of the letter, and his actions afterwards, will provide the conspirators with hilarious laughter. This customarily solemn-suited man will appear to Olivia wearing yellow stockings, cross-gartered. This customarily solemn-faced man will appear smiling to Olivia. This customarily solemn-thinking man will, suffering from delusions of grandeur, attempt to flirt with Olivia.

How good the plan is we discover when next we see Malvolio. He has not seen the letter yet, but obviously Maria has been shrewd enough to be cognizant of his inmost thoughts. When we next see him, he is meditating—day-dreaming would be a better term—on his future. He envisions himself married to the Countess Olivia. If we examine the text closely, we can readily see that love for Olivia has nothing to do with his yearnings. If love entered into the situation at all, we might be inclined to feel some sympathy for him, but his desire for marriage is not motivated by love. He is motivated solely by a yearning for the power that a husband of the Countess, a Count Malvolio, might possess. He would have power to give orders to the Countess' uncle, his mortal enemy, Sir Toby Belch; he would have power to control the household and give orders to the Fabians and the Festes and the Marias who now tend to flout him; things would be done his way. As he envisions this happy circumstance, he naturally makes derogatory comments about Sir Toby. If we, aware of the humor in the situation of the biter being bitten, laugh at the concealed Toby's reactions to Malvolio's comments, we laugh more loudly at Malvolio's presumption because we know that Olivia's affections do not incline in his direction. We laugh, too, at his gaucherie when, in his day-dreaming, he makes the classic mistake of confusing the present with the future: "I frown the while, and perchance wind up my watch, or play with my—some rich jewel." The "my" and the hesitation that follows it are important in this connection. Malvolio forgets momentarily that as Count Malvolio he would no longer be wearing his chain, the menial steward's badge of office. It is a natural mistake, to be sure, but we laugh at it because it is a mistake growing out of presumption.

But all this takes place before he finds Maria's carefully phrased letter. The timing here is most important. Had he been led to such envisionings by the discovery of the letter and the ambiguous words which it contains, we might feel sorry for him. As the circumstance exists, however, we do not feel sorry for him at all. The confidence man's cliché, "You can't cheat an honest man," helps us here. Malvolio had yearnings for power before he ever saw the letter. He asked to be duped. His thoughts were channeled in the proper direction before the trick was played on him. The letter merely confirmed his thoughts. Why shouldn't we laugh at him? Why should we sympathize with him? He asked for it.

So he attires himself as the letter suggested; he alters his solemn countenance and appears smiling when Olivia wants him. He couldn't have chosen a worse time to slough off his solemn attitude. Olivia had wanted him because she is despondent, and Malvolio, normally "sad and civil . . . suits well for a servant with my fortunes." So he prances in, gay, flirting, full of ambiguous and veiled reference to the letter about which Olivia knows nothing. It is little wonder that his behavior and appearance cause Olivia to believe that he is a victim of midsummer madness. Kind and gentle, although despondent, she asks that some of her people take care of Malvolio and she asks that Sir Toby look to him. Her reaction to his situation pleases the dupe. If no lower member of the household than Sir Toby is to look after him, surely his dreams have not been in vain, surely nothing can come between him and the full prospect of his hopes. So self-centered is his imagination that he is unable to realize that if Olivia's orders please him, they please Toby and his group even more. The nuisance, the villain, is now in their clutches. They treat him as a madman; according to the benevolent custom of the day, they throw him into a dark room, all the while abjuring him to renounce the devil who assuredly has possessed him. Once he is safely confined, they take this wonderful opportunity to play pranks on him, to torment him, to send Feste in guise of a priest to reprove him. But all will come out in the end. Feste brings him pen, ink, and paper. From the depths of his self-pity, Malvolio composes a letter part pleading, part cajoling, part injured. Feste delivers the letter to Olivia. Olivia, who has always thought kindly of Malvolio, but who always thought of him not as a husband but as a good and faithful servant, sees to it that he is released. Fabian tells all, carefully shielding Maria, as a gentleman should do, and taking all the blame on his shoulders and on the broad shoulders of Sir Toby. He does so, it must be confessed, after Olivia has assured Malvolio that he will be both plantiff and judge in his own case. Nevertheless, Fabian's speech is important. It tells us some important information, and it gives a fair account of the proceedings:

> Good madam, hear me speak,
> And let no quarrel, nor no brawl to come,
> Taint the condition of this present hour,
> Which I have wond'red at. In hope it shall not
> Most freely I confess myself and Toby
> Set this device against Malvolio here,
> Upon some stubborn and discourteous parts
> We had conceiv'd against him. Maria writ
> The letter, at Sir Toby's great importance,
> In recompense whereof he hath married her.
> How with a sportful malice it was follow'd

> May rather pluck on laughter than revenge,
> If that the injuries be justly weigh'd
> That have on both sides pass'd.

Fabian here demonstrates the essential difference between the sympathetic and antagonistic comic character. The plot was Maria's from the start, but he takes the blame on himself and on Sir Toby who, despite his wounds, is well able to bear it. He demonstrates completely that both sides have been wronged, and that the whole affair, seen in the proper light, is cause for laughter, not revenge. Certainly his approach is reasonable but, conciliatory though it may be, it brings from Malvolio only the bitter exit line, "I'll be reveng'd on the whole pack of you!"

How, then, are we to feel about Malvolio? The answer seems simple. If this is a play about music, he is the discord. If this is a play about laughter, he is the frown. If this is a play about unselfish, romantic love, he, selfishly, loves only himself. Despite Maurice Evans' television version of *Twelfth Night*, despite reputable critics like Mark Van Doren, Malvolio is not the center, the focal point of this romantic comedy, any more than Parolles is the center of *All's Well That Ends Well*, or Don John the center of *Much Ado About Nothing*. Malvolio is a minor obstacle in the path of true love. If the purpose of *Twelfth Night* is to get Viola married to Duke Orsino, and Olivia married to Sebastian, and Maria married to Sir Toby, why do we need Malvolio? We need him to laugh at, because we laugh with all the rest. We laugh with Feste, with Sir Toby, with Maria, with Fabian, even with the Duke in his romantic melancholia, and with Viola in her almost insurmountable problem. We laugh at Malvolio. He is opposed to culture and grace and laughter and joy and music—all the things that we care for. So we laugh at him. In a world of unselfish love, he is selfish. So we laugh at him. We don't have to call him a Puritan; we just have to call him a kill-joy, a time-pleaser, a self-seeker. He exits with our laughter ringing in his ears. If Olivia, the tender-hearted, thinks him notoriously abused, and if Duke Orsino, suddenly practical, wants peace made with him so that he can discover more information about Viola's friendly and helpful Captain, we don't mind. We really don't want Malvolio destroyed; we merely want him to be taught a lesson. If he can't learn, so much the worse for him. There will still be Illyria filled with frank and open love; and there will still be Feste making jokes, getting in scrapes, singing his lovely songs; and there will still be Sir Toby with his hatred for unfilled cans. What more do we need than love and laughter and song and conviviality? So we laugh at Malvolio's final exit because he has been foiled in his desire to substitute self-love for romantic love, a serious mien for frank and open laughter, and the conning of politic authors for the gaiety of song and conviviality.

Parolles, Mr. Applegate, Harry Brock, and Malvolio do not, of course, exhaust the roster of comic antagonists in dramatic literature. They are merely representatives of their type, but if we want to understand dramatic comedy we must understand them. I suggest that if there is a physiological theory of tragedy, and Aristotle's *Poetics* with its emphasis on catharsis is at least one such theory, then it is equally possible to have a physiological theory of comedy. This theory would also emphasize catharsis, but not catharsis of the emotions of pity and terror. The emotions that we seek to purge in comedy are those of scorn and mockery. We do not scorn, we cannot mock, the sympathetic comic character. We certainly are able to scorn and to mock the comic antagonist, the comic villain. Strangely enough, the tragic hero and the comic villain have some things in common. Both are over-reachers; both suffer from hubris; both try to possess more power than is rightfully theirs. The tragic hero is destroyed by the operation of nemesis; the comic villain is frustrated through the mockery of our laughter. The audience of a comedy does not ask that the villain be destroyed; it merely asks that he be foiled. If, like Parolles, he has a possibility of reformation, we are pleased, but not so much that we want to sympathize with him. If, like Mr. Applegate, Harry Brock, or Malvolio, he has no prospect of reformation we do not really mind. For then we can feel superior to him, and we can scorn not only his over-reaching, but also his intellectual blindness, his stiff-necked arrogance. This feeling of superiority is germane to Aristotle's theory of tragedy; it is equally germane to this theory of comedy. For we can seldom, unless we are blind, feel superior to the sympathetic comic character; we can always feel superior to the comic antagonist. And when we leave the theater or put down the copy of the play, we can have a feeling akin to that of the Greek audience which had seen an Aeschylean or Sophoclean tetralogy. The Greek audience, if we are to believe Aristotle, felt superior to the plight of the tragic hero. It reasoned, "Here is this man, noble, even regal. If such terrible things can happen to him through frailty and error, my problems are not so bad after all. I'm really better off than he." When we have seen a comic villain foiled, we can feel superior to him, wondering, if he does show symptoms of reformation, what ever made him so stupid in the first place; congratulating ourselves, if he shows no signs of reformation, on being less stupid, less narrow of vision than he. And we do not mind that the villain has not been destroyed for we generally feel, smugly perhaps, that it will serve him right to go on living with himself. His narrow-visioned pride, his selfishness, his humorlessness, his frustrations should provide him with the kind of company he deserves. The villain has become our butt—the sympathetic comic characters have seen to that—and he has served his purpose admirably well. The bogey man in the children's fairy tales takes fear with him when he is revealed as merely a shadow of evil; the comic villain takes our scorn and our mockery with him when he is revealed as easily foiled, easily frustrated. It is good that he does so. The scorn and the mockery which we so frequently feel should be directed against ourselves have found another target. We can be pleased, we can be content, we can almost feel a little self-satisfied—until the next time we do something foolish.

"You remember the time I knocked Chicago Molly down?"
"Why, you didn't knock her down—I did."
"Well, I started kicking her first."
—W. C. FIELDS in *My Little Chickadee*

Cruelty and comedy (1): "You beat your pate, and fancy wit will come."

The curtain rises on Act II, scene v of a great tragedy. A beautiful and imperious queen is discovered with her retinue. She is moody, irritable; she seems not to know what to do with herself; time hangs heavily on her hands. She is waiting, as we soon discover, for a message from her loved one who is far away across the sea. First she calls for music, "moody food of us that trade in love," but even before the first notes sound she has already changed her mind. Now she wants to play billiards. She asks one of her attendant ladies to play with her, but the lady, pleading a sore arm, begs off, and suggests that the queen play with her eunuch. The eunuch is willing enough to play, but by the time the queen has taken a moment to voice a mildly bawdy joke at his expense, her mood changes once more and she decides to go fishing. The thought of fishing is satisfying to her momentarily sadistic bent. She intends to "betray" the fish by having her music play far off. Her hook shall pierce their slimy jaws, and she shall call every one of them by the name of her lover as she draws them up, saying, " 'Ah, ha! y'are caught!' " Her lady-in-waiting reminds her of the time that the queen and her lover had gone fishing and wagered on the outcome. At that time one of the queen's divers had put an old salted and dried fish on her lover's hook, and the whole retinue had laughed at his discomfiture. The queen remembers that she had laughed him out of patience, and then laughed him into patience, and then drunk him to his bed. Not satisfied with that, she had dressed him in her own head-dress and mantle, and she had put on his victorious sword. At this point in the reminiscence, the long-awaited messenger arrives. He tries to give his message, but the queen's impetuosity is such that he can scarcely get two words out (or, rather, one word repeated) before she is interrupting, imagining all sorts of dire circumstances that have afflicted her lover. Finally, after many attempts and many interruptions, the messenger is able to deliver his message. It contains worse news than she had imagined. It would have been bad enough for her to have heard that her lover had been captured or was dead; it is worse to hear that he has been married to another woman. She is unable to accept the news with equanimity. We hadn't expected that she would. We might have expected that she would fall into a fit of hysterics, but she goes much further than that. She knocks the messenger down; she strikes him; she drags him up and down the room by his hair; she draws a knife on him. The messenger prudently runs away. The audience imprudently laughs, as it has been laughing all through the scene. The audience knows that it is watching the tragedy of *Antony and Cleopatra*, yet it laughs. The audience knows that it is watching a scene of cruelty and brutality, yet it laughs.

This audience is not composed exclusively of sadists. This is a very sophisticated audience attending a performance of one of Shakespeare's most sophisticated plays. It probably knows what Aristotle has said about tragedy. It may even know that Aristotle has said of comedy:

> It is an imitation of men worse than the average; worse, however, not as regards any and every sort of fault, but only as regards one particular kind, the Ridiculous, which is a species of the Ugly. The Ridiculous may be defined as a mistake or deformity, not productive of pain or harm to others; the mask, for instance, that excites laughter, is something ugly and distorted without causing pain.

But what Aristotle has said doesn't seem to help very much in this situation. The queen probably has acted in a ridiculous manner, but she has caused pain or the appearance of pain. The audience is in a dilemma. It undoubtedly feels a sense of concern, a sense of sympathy for the messenger who merely reports the news; he does not, after all, create it: "Gracious madam, I that do bring the news made not the match." It may even feel a sense of sympathy for the betrayed queen. It laughs, nonetheless, because it has witnessed a cruel and brutal comic scene. Why it laughs at cruelty and brutality is another matter, a matter which requires much thought.

For if we fail to analyze closely, cruelty and comedy seem to have little in common: one causes pain, the other pleasure; one causes moans, the other laughter; one causes sorrow, the other joy. Yet, empirically, they must have something in common, for cruelty and brutality have frequently been used as an occasion for comedy, as a source of laughter. We see them at work together in the beating that Strepsiades receives at the hands of his son Phidippides in *The Clouds*; we laugh at the wonderful domestic battle between Noah and his wife in the Wakefield *Noah* play; we laugh as the rascally Mak gets tossed in a blanket by the duped shepherds in *Secunda Pastorum*; we see them, too, in the beatings that the clever servant comes, resignedly, poutingly, to accept as his due, whether his name is Sosia in *The Amphitruo*, Dromio in *The Comedy of Errors*, Fag in *The Rivals*, or Harpo Marx as he ministers to the needs of the irascible Sig Rumann in *A Night in Casablanca*. The means and implements used by the beaters may and do change—one need only recall the open hand, the fist, the foot, the bastinado, the whip, Sig Rumann's rapier, Chaplin's cane, Mike Sacks's inflated bladder, Mack Swain's bed slat, and Mabel Normand's custard pie—but the beating remains an anticipated and comic constant.

Frequently one beating, comic though it may be, is merely the beginning of a series of beatings, each one funnier than the last. The father beats the son, the son beats the servant, the servant beats the scullery or errand boy, and the boy, finding no human being below him in the order of things, promptly kicks the dog. Bergson would probably call such a piling up of circumstance the Snowball Effect. Sheridan, in *The Rivals*, doesn't bother to name it. He merely uses the device for comedy. Captain Absolute and his father, Sir Anthony Absolute, have had, as their names might suggest, a violent disagreement. Obviously the father and son, despite their name, have been too well bred to resort to blows; threats and vituperation are more their stock in trade. The father's exit lines indicate the mood: "I'll disown you, I'll disinherit you, I'll unget you! and damn me! if ever I call you Jack again!" Although there were no blows, blows were not far from the old man's mind. Fag, the servant, enters at this point, and tells the Captain and us the Audience what old Sir Anthony did after he left the room:

> He comes downstairs eight or ten steps at a time—muttering, growling, and thumping the bannisters all the way: I, and the cook's dog, stand bowing at the door—rap! he gives me a stroke on the head with his cane; bids me carry that to my master, then kicking the poor turnspit into the area, damns us all for a puppy triumvirate!

The Captain, still angered by his interview with his father, orders Fag to cease his impertinence, and pushes him aside roughly as he leaves the room. That leaves Fag alone for a moment on the stage, and he takes the opportunity to wax philosophical—until an errand boy arrives:

> FAG: So! Sir Anthony trims my master: he is afraid to reply to his father—then vents his spleen on poor Fag! When one is vexed by one person, to revenge oneself on another, who happens to come in the way, is the vilest injustice! Ah! it shows the worst temper—the basest—
>
> *Enter Errand Boy*
>
> BOY: Mr. Fag! Mr. Fag! your master calls you.
>
> FAG: Well, you little dirty puppy, you need not bawl so!—The meanest disposition! the—
>
> BOY: Quick! quick, Mr. Fag.
>
> FAG: Quick! quick! You impudent jackanapes! am I to be commanded by you too? you little, impertinent, insolent, kitchen-bred—
>
> *Exit kicking and beating him.*

Why do we laugh at this scene when we read it or see it presented on the stage? There are probably many reasons but, when we examine the circumstances closely, three stand out. In the first place, Sir Anthony is of choleric temperament. He has been crossed, and no one crosses him with impunity. The words he has used to cudgel his son are merely substitutes— and not very satisfactory ones to a person of his disposition— for the blows that he wants to strike. But how can a man strike a fully grown son, particularly when this son is a captain? Yet the blow must be struck. So, when he hits Fag on the head with his cane, he makes it clear to Fag and the audience that the blow was intended for his son. Fag, then, becomes the innocent bystander who receives the blow intended for another. Perhaps this does not seem comic, but it may be pertinent to point out that many of the pie-throwing routines in Mack Sennett moving pictures depend upon just this device for comic effect. Chaplin is very fond of it, and he doesn't always rely upon pie throwing. He does use pie in *A Night in the Show*, but he uses ice cream in *By the Sea*, a mop in *Triple Trouble*, a sword in *Carmen*, and a fist in *His New Job*. The device, or something resembling it, appears in almost every two-reeler he made, as it appears in many of the Laurel and Hardy two-reelers.

When Jule Styne and Sammy Cahn wrote the music and lyrics for the Stephen Longstreet musical comedy *High Button Shoes*, they wrote one song, *The Innocent Standerby*, which, to the best of my knowledge, never appeared in the show. It is unfortunate that the song disappeared in rehearsal, for it is pertinent in this connection, particularly the first eight bars:

> When two guys argue and quarrel,
> Who gets it in the eye?
> Not the fellow who started the quarrel,
> But the innocent standerby.

But we need not confine ourselves to Mack Sennett, Charlie Chaplin, Laurel and Hardy, and *High Button Shoes*. The device is a staple of Jacobean and Restoration drama. It appears in Roman comedy when the braggart soldier, shown up as a coward, goes home and beats his servant. Nor does the innocent standerby have to be animate. In one of Jolita's *Little Eve* cartoons, the first panel shows Little Eve berating her silent husband; the next panels show him walking up the stairs to the attic; the last panel shows him revengefully kicking her dress form. Nor do we need to confine ourselves to comedy. The device of the innocent bystander exists in the garb of tragic irony when Cinna the poet is destroyed by the mob in *Julius Caesar*, when Macduff's wife and children are murdered in *Macbeth*, when Satan, in *Paradise Lost*, unable to get back at God, decides to seduce Adam and Eve, two of the lower members of God's creation. But the device most often appears in comedy. When it does appear in tragedy we get not true tragedy but ironic horror.

But the innocent-bystander routine, comic though it may be, is only one of the reasons we laugh at the Fag episode. Consider another aspect of the scene. The scene contains an inevitable, though possibly illogical, series of events: the father abuses the son, and the servant in lieu of the son; the son abuses the servant, too; the servant abuses the errand boy; and the errand boy, presumably, abuses the cook's dog. We have found such a series comic since we were children. *The Farmer in the Dell* and *Old Macdonald Had a Farm* are merely variations on the theme. *The House that Jack Built*, particularly in its sixth stanza, demonstrates the technique admirably:

> This is the cow with the crumpled horn,
> That tossed the dog,
> That worried the cat,
> That killed the rat,
> That ate the malt,
> That lay in the house that Jack built.

The Hebrew Passover Seder has in it (significantly at the end so that the children who like it will stay awake during the rest of the service) the *Chad Gadya* which contains a series of violences, to be sure, but also an insistence upon the omnipotence of God:

> One kid which my father bought for two zuzim:
> And a cat came and ate the kid,
> And a dog came and bit the cat,
> And a stick came and hit the dog,
> And a fire came and consumed the stick,

And water came and extinguished the fire,
And an ox came and drank the water,
And the shochet came and slaughtered the ox,
And the Angel of Death came and killed the shochet,
And the Holy One Blessed be He came and destroyed the
Angel of Death.

As can be readily seen, the *Chad Gadya* contains very little instructional matter in comparison to the great amount of pleasurable sugar coating. The little instruction that is present tends to fade into insignificance when it is mentioned that after each line of the verse the same refrain line is sung. And what is the refrain line? Has anything new been added? The answer is, of course, no. The refrain line is merely the repetition of the first two words of the song: "Chad gadya, chad gadya." Certainly the song's primary purpose is to provide, by means of a series of violent incidents, by means of repetition of the same syllables, a reason for laughter, a source of pleasure. This may seem Bergsonian, particularly when we think of his principles of "repetition," "inversion," and the "reciprocal interference of series," but it is only superficially so. When Bergson speaks of "repetition," he means "coincidence"; when he speaks of "inversion," he means "the robber robbed," or "the biter bitten"; when he speaks of "the reciprocal interference of series," he means *a situation . . . [which] belongs simultaneously to two altogether independent series of events and is capable of being interpreted in two entirely different meanings at the same time.*" In other words, Bergson is dealing with problems that are far more complex than the rather simple one proposed to us by our series of events.

In addition to the innocent-bystander device and the series-of-events technique, there is a third reason that the Fag episode is comic. And if Bergson doesn't help us too much with the second, he certainly helps us with the third. Fag has been saying, "When one is vexed by one person, to revenge oneself on another, who happens to come in the way, is the vilest injustice!" when the errand boy comes into the room. Fag immediately forgets his moralizing, forgets his philosophy, and begins to beat and kick the boy. He does so, of course, not for anything the boy has done (although he does try rationalization on this point) but simply because he has been beaten and shoved by Sir Anthony and Captain Absolute. To order an inferior to follow advice, not example, is a common enough, though deplorable, practice among teachers and parents. To reason a course of conduct and then do the opposite is a common practice of mankind. As Bergson says, "It is not uncommon for a comic character to condemn in general terms a certain line of conduct and immediately afterwards afford an example of it himself: for instance, M. Jourdain's teacher of philosophy [in *The Would-Be Gentleman*] flying into a passion after inveighing against anger." Many other examples could be added to Fag and M. Jourdain: practically all the characters in *Love's Labour's Lost*, but particularly the King and Armado, are guilty; Rosalind in *As You Like It* is guilty; Beatrice and Benedick in *Much Ado About Nothing* are guilty; I am guilty, you are guilty, he, she, or it is guilty.

Perhaps, then, it has been demonstrated that a simple comic beating is not so simple after all. There are many reasons why we laugh at a stage beating, and the three which I have given do not exhaust all of the possibilities. Nor do I believe that we are sadists when we laugh at the messenger in *Antony and Cleopatra* or at Fag in *The Rivals*. I do believe, however, the primary reason we laugh in each instance is that the beating is undeserved. If the victim had done something wrong, we might believe that the beating is both deserved and real. Since the victim had done nothing wrong, we permit ourselves to take refuge in the theatrical bromide: "they make love in jest, they poison in jest"; and we add one of our own: "they beat in jest." Since the beating is undeserved, it is obviously unreal. We can, therefore, laugh; we do not have to take action.

Perhap it was something of this nature, something of the essential unreality which underlies comic brutality, that Harold Ross had in mind in an episode mentioned by James Thurber in his book *The Years With Ross:*

> He [Ross] was wary of fatality in drawings, sharing Paul Nash's conviction that "not even Americans can make death funny," and when Carl Rose, in 1932, submitted a picture of a fencer cutting off his opponent's head and crying "Touché!" Ross thought it was too bloody and gruesome, and asked Rose to let me have a swing at it, because "Thurber's people have no blood. You can put their heads back on and they're good as new." It worked out that way. Nobody was horrified.

And few people have been horrified by Charles Addams' cartoons with their emphasis on the supernatural, on organized mayhem, on the bizarre, on the exotic. Do we willingly suspend disbelief for the time that it takes us to smile, or laugh? I doubt it. We smile or laugh because disbelief is not suspended. We know we are laughing at the unreal, not the real. We are the sophisticated, so we laugh. The unsophisticated might give forth a shriek of horror. It is too simple to say, as Al Capp does, "All comedy is based on man's delight in man's inhumanity to man." Even all of Mr. Capp's comedy is not based on that premise. His Shmoos, for example, were the source of gentle laughter before he found it necessary to kill them all off. We certainly do not shed tears over a creature that wants to die, is determined to die, finds happiness in dying, if someone looks at it hungrily.

Before we leave the subject of comic beatings, it might be well to point out what a modern master of slapstick had to say on the subject. Ezra Goodman once interviewed Mack Sennett and published the result of that interview in the New York *Times.* Among other enlightening things, this is what he had to say:

> What would Sennett say were the ingredients of successful screen slapstick? "Brevity is one," he holds. Another is "controlled

pandemonium." "But," he emphasized, "there is one slapstick rule that is absolutely essential. Never hit mother in the face with a pie. Give it to the mother-in-law, but not mother."

Mr. Sennett's language may be slightly inelegant, but his point is beautifully clear. He holds, as do so many other thinkers on the subject of comedy, that there are some subjects that comedy should not touch. Even so learned a thinker as James Thurber has maintained that ". . . major blasphemies have no place in comedy." Leaving aside the fact that blasphemy does not admit of degree, we find few subjects from mother to God that comedy has not touched, and successfully too. Sostrata, the mother of Lucrezia, in Machiavelli's *Mandragola*, is certainly made an object of mirth. The Lawd in Marc Connelly's *Green Pastures* is frequently treated with what must be to the devout unpardonable freedom. Indeed, much comedy depends on treating a serious subject with levity. Certainly war is a serious subject, but among many other examples we have *What Price Glory?*, Chaplin's *Shoulder Arms*, Keaton's *The General*, Bill Mauldin's cartoons, and *Stalag* 17 treating actual combat and imprisonment with a light touch. The political leaders and rulers of great countries should be taken seriously, but we remember with pleasure and delight the annual Gridiron Club Dinner, *Of Thee I Sing*, Chaplin's *The Great Dictator*, and *Love's Labour's Lost*. We can almost say that if a subject is unable to bear our laughter, it does not merit our serious consideration. Man's attitude toward proper objects of mirth has changed little in the millennia that elapsed between the homeric laughter of the gods at Hephaestus bustling from room to room and the laughter of the average man who could purchase a newspaper and enjoy the sight of a dwarf perched on the elephantine thighs of the late J. P. Morgan.

It should be clear by now that beatings are not the only form of physical cruelty that we have in comedy. Restraint of freedom is certainly a form of physical cruelty, and such restraint has frequently been a source of laughter. Malvolio in *Twelfth Night*, receiving the standard Elizabethan treatment for suspected lunatics, is incarcerated in a dark room; the audience laughs at him. The man or woman in puritan New England who had committed a peccadillo was placed in the stocks; the passersby, we are told, laughed at the sight. In Charlie Chaplin's *Work*, Charlie's slave-driving and irascible boss gets his head stuck in a bucket of wallpaper paste; the audience howls at his discomfiture. Sig Rumann in the Marx Brothers' film *A Night at the Opera* plays the role of a pompous impresario who loses most of his clothes and gets locked in a closet when he attempts to block the course of true love and hilarious laughter; the audience enjoys his predicament. It may well be argued that all these examples, even that of the puritan man or woman, are comic antagonists or comic butts, and that we would naturally laugh at anything which causes them annoyance or pain. That's true enough, but we also laugh at the situation of the sympathetic comic character whose freedom is restrained. And there are ways to restrain that do not involve the locked door, the iron bars, the stocks, or the oubliette. Clothes can be a restraining force. In *As You Like It*, Rosalind must wear male attire. Her transvestitism causes her many problems, problems that merit our laughter. A young girl falls in love with her; her father fails to recognize her (a minor matter, to be sure, for as she says, "But what talk we of fathers when there is such a man as Orlando?"); her true love, and this is the major difficulty, doesn't recognize her either. She is unable to act as she wants to act, speak as she wants to speak. Clothes have restrained her freedom as much as the locked closet door restrained Sig Rumann's freedom, as much as the dark room restrained Malvolio's freedom. Of course, her restraints are dissolved in the end just as Malvolio's are, just as Sig Rumann's are, just as the similar restraints of

Viola in *Twelfth Night* are. But she is a sympathetic comic character, and her freedom has been restrained, and the audience has laughed.

Not clothes but a machine restrains Chaplin's freedom in *Modern Times*. He becomes its victim, its servant, its slave. The cog wheel catches him up and makes him, temporarily, a component part of the diabolical mechanism: the automatic feeder feeds him nuts and bolts. He has no freedom of motion; he has no freedom of thought. By the time that he escapes from it, the machine has imposed upon him one reflex action: with a huge wrench he proceeds, temporarily deranged, to tighten everything in sight, no matter how slightly it resembles a nut. Like Pavlov's dogs, he has been conditioned, and the audience, primitive or sophisticated, conditioned or unconditioned, laughs at this sympathetic character whose freedom has been restrained.

While clothes and machines, bear traps and paste buckets can restrain freedom, the obvious restraint is the jail cell or the prospect of a jail cell. No one who saw it will ever forget Willie Howard's plaintive but fruitless cry from the cell to his lawyer, "Pay the two dollars." Phil Silvers, in his television role of Sergeant Bilko, frequently found himself in the guardhouse. One episode is germane to this discussion. Colonel Hall has passed an anti-gambling ordinance. Bilko naturally violates the ordinance. He is, as might be expected, confined. Confinement of this most rugged of all individualists would inevitably be a source of comedy, but this confinement is more than ordinarily comic because he has sought it. He has conceived a diabolically clever plan. If things go according to his plan, Sergeants Grover and Ritzik, his two favorite poker victims, will be confined with him. In the guardhouse with nothing else to do, he will have infinite leisure to fleece them. His plan goes awry. He is confined, to be sure, but they are forcibly prevented from joining him. At this point in the script it is difficult to determine which is the most comic: their attempts to get in the guardhouse (no victims ever fought harder to be slaughtered), Bilko's attempts to get out, or the attempts of all three to play poker while he is in and they are out and the military policemen are attempting to restore order. To argue that the audience is not laughing at cruelty, to argue that it is laughing at a magnificent example of the punishment fitting the crime, is to miss the point. Bilko's freedom is restrained. He epitomizes the free spirit. Any type of physical restraint is cruel, is brutal, both to him and to his sympathetic audience. That other sources of humor are present in the episode, I freely admit. The inflexibility of the official mind is clearly portrayed by the military policemen. The eagerness of gulls to be gulled is clearly portrayed by Grover and Ritzik. As mentioned above, Bilko's predicament may well be considered an excellent example of the biter being bitten, because he has sought the imprisonment. But the physical restraint of the free spirit is the primary source of comedy in the episode.

The practical joke is another form of cruelty that frequently causes laughter. If you were to ask fifty people if they find practical jokes funny, all fifty would deny that they do, and vehemently. At least forty-nine of them will laugh when they see one. The minor reservation is necessary here because the victim rarely, if ever, laughs. Our present degree of sophistication causes us to maintain that we frown, not laugh, at practical jokes. The practical joke, we say, is low brow, is infra dig. Yet practical jokes are not now and never have been confined to the low brow. There are such elaborate, high brow, literary practical jokes as "Bunburying" in *The Importance of Being Earnest,* the disguised Rosalind's treatment of the love-sick Orlando in *As You Like It,* and the horning of Messer Nicia in *Mandragola.* Our sophisticates generally laugh at these episodes. They will laugh, too, at the clever administration of a hot foot, the dextrous removal of a chair as the victim attempts to sit, the ingenious mechanical contrivance that causes a bucket of water to inundate a victim as he opens a door. They won't admit laughing at such incidents, even though they do so, unless you follow the advice of H. Allen Smith and refer to them not as "practical jokes," but as "pranks."

Indeed, most practical jokes, literary or non-literary, do not deal in physical pain; they deal, instead, in emotional pain, in emotional brutality. But with all our newly acquired knowledge of psychosomatic medicine, we should hesitate before we draw any sharp line of demarcation between emotional and physical pain. For the practical joke, physical and emotional, has been a staple of literary comedy from *The Clouds* through *Love's Labour's Lost* and *The Jumping Frog of Calaveras County* to Sam and Bella Spewack's *Kiss Me, Kate!* And there are merely differences in degree, not in kind, when Bill Calhoun signs Fred Graham's name to a $10,000 I.O.U. in *Kiss Me, Kate!*, or when the Princess of France and her ladies exchange favors so that they can confuse the King of Navarre and his gentlemen in *Love's Labour's Lost*, or when Joe the Joker administers a hot foot in Damon Runyon's short story *Sense of Humor.*

Mention of *The Jumping Frog of Calaveras County* brings to mind the pertinent fact that the victim of comic brutality or the practical joke need not always be human. The popularity of the Donald Duck and the Tom and Jerry cartoons is proof of that. Indeed, the victim of comic brutality need not even be animate. The *Little Eve* cartoon mentioned above provides proof. Both Jimmy Durante and Harpo Marx cause laughter, despite the occasional twinge of regret that stirs in the breast of the music lover when they destroy a piano before the eyes of the audience. The destruction of a golf club or a billiard cue following a poor shot has frequently caused laughter both on the stage and in life. And W. C. Fields, operating on the theory that you can create comedy when an object that the audience expects to break merely bends, capitalized on this point with a succession of canes, billiard cues, and golf clubs. Even Fields was not totally immune to the destructive infection. In *The Barber Shop*, Fields is represented as owning a bass violin called "Lena." A man comes in and tries to sell him another bass violin which is, according to the owner's nomenclature, masculine. Unsuccessful in his attempt at a sale, he asks Fields's permission to leave his bass fiddle in the barber shop while he does some shopping. At the end of the two-reeler, Fields discovers that the two bass violins have propagated a litter of violins. In paternal outrage he destroys the masculine intruder as he kicks it out of his shop.

Despite the plethora of golf clubs and canes and pianos and fiddles that populate comedy, the victim of comic brutality is most often human or possessed of human characteristics. Al Capp's *L'il Abner* with its cast of comic brutes is a case in point. So, too, is George Willard's *Moon Mullins*, which presents in the characters of Willie and Mamie a twentieth-century version of the Wakefield *Noah* play. Of course, there is a major, twentieth-century difference: Willie, unlike Noah, never wins either argument or fight. To mention comic strips and not to mention George Herriman's *Krazy Kat* would be to lose critical franchise. *Krazy Kat* is full of poetic language, classical allusion, universal symbolism. Yet in this strip a unique form of violence is raised to high comic art. The three principal characters in the strip, Krazy Kat, Ignatz Mouse, and Offissa Pupp, have already been celebrated by such formidable intellects as Gilbert Seldes and E. E. Cummings. It would be difficult to disagree with Seldes and Cummings—even if I wanted to, which I don't—but we should not lose sight of the fact that the primary source of humor in the cartoon is a brick flying through the air. The brick has been hurled with deadly accuracy by Ignatz; its target is the loving head of Krazy, who must not, despite her pleasure at being hit, be called a masochist; the task of preventing the flight of the brick or, as is most often the case, punishing the hurler, is Offissa Pupp's. Certainly there are other aspects of comedy in the strip. It seems contrary to nature that a cat should love a mouse or that a dog should love a cat, but that's the way Herriman's world is. Cummings explains the situation as well as anyone can explain the inexplicable:

> Two of the protagonists are easily recognized as a cynical brick-throwing mouse and a sentimental policeman-dog. The third protagonist—whose ambiguous gender doesn't disguise the good news that here comes our heroine—may be described as a humbly poetic, gently clownlike, supremely innocent, and illimitably affectionate creature (slightly resembling a child's drawing of a cat, but gifted with the secret grace and obvious clumsiness of a penguin on terra firma) who is never so happy as when egoist-mouse, thwarting altruist-dog, hits her in the head with a brick. Dog hates mouse and worships "cat," mouse despises "cat" and hates dog, "cat" hates no one and loves mouse. . . . Joy is her [Krazy's] destiny: and joy comes through Ignatz—via Offissa Pupp; since it is our villain's loathing for law which gives him the strength of ten when he hurls his blissyielding brick. Let's not forget that. And let's be perfectly sure about something else. Even if Offissa Pupp should go crazy and start chasing Krazy, and even if Krazy should go crazy and start chasing Ignatz, and even if crazy Krazy should swallow crazy Ignatz and crazy Offissa Pupp should swallow Krazy and it was the millennium—there'd still be the brick. And (having nothing else to swallow) Offissa Pupp would then swallow the brick. Whereupon, as the brick hit Krazy, Krazy would be happy.

As Cummings says, "There'd still be the brick," and this brick has lost many of its normal connotations. It is not designed to be part of a noble edifice, or of a body-and-spirit-warming fireplace, or even of a herringbone-pattern sidewalk. It is designed purely as a weapon and, as a weapon, it is, in Cummings' word, "blissyielding." How much more can you ask of an inanimate object? This brick is, in so many ways, superior to Chaplin's cane or Fields's billiard cue or Durante's piano. In *Krazy Kat* cruelty and brutality cause a type of laughter that we normally do not associate with violence: one of the highest forms of comedy, the comedy of joy. James Feibleman in his book *In Praise of Comedy* lists the names of comedy in descending order: Joy, Divine Comedy, Humour, Irony, Satire, Sarcasm, Wit, and Scorn. As Feibleman is aware, no one will agree completely with the order of his list, but he has done a brave service in preparing the order. Just as an example, I might prefer placing Divine Comedy higher than Joy, and placing Wit higher than Sarcasm, but there is some merit to his list. Certainly (remember Cummings' word "blissyielding") *Krazy Kat* belongs in the Joy category; normally comedy of brutality would be placed on a far lower plane.

There are, then, many forms of cruelty that cause laughter and comedy, and the comedy that is created is not confined to any one aspect. Cruelty can create high comedy as well as farce, sophistication as well as slapstick. The mention of farce and slapstick, however, brings to mind the formidable comic chases included in every Marx Brothers or W. C. Fields moving picture. These chases involve not only the participants but also the spectators. So comic are these chases that it might well be argued that the invention of the automobile and the motion-picture camera created a new dimension in comic horror. That there are comic chases in plays that antedate the automobile and the motion-picture camera, I am well aware; that these earlier chases, even such a brilliant one as that in *The Birds*, are limited in technique and effect, I insist. To see a chase in a Keystone Comedy or in Chaplin's *The Kid*, or in *The Bank Dick* or in *The Big Store*, is to laugh at dangers narrowly missed, to thumb one's nose at death and destruction, to achieve once more—if only vicariously—the splendid exhilaration that we knew as children when, with shirts stuffed with stolen apples, we outdistanced the heavy-footed, irascible owner of the tree. But it may be argued that the chase is not brutal or cruel. The sympathetic comic characters, admittedly, generally escape, but the threat of cruelty and brutality is always present. Fear of cruelty, fear of brutality can be as potent in evoking laughter as the fact of cruelty or the fact of brutality. As Buster Keaton has said, "The best way to get a laugh is to create a genuine thrill and then relieve the tension with comedy." The chase, then, is generally more comic if the crack-up at the end is avoided. Here is one case when the will is genuinely preferred to the deed.

Along with the chase as a source of the comic we should mention the sick joke, the cruel joke, the Bloody Mary—call it what you will—that a few years ago swept the country into its mephitic embrace. While the comic chase of the motion picture is a new dimension in comedy, the sick joke most definitely is not. It is older than Aristophanes and obligingly appears on the scene whenever the sophisticates of an age, be they the courtiers of Caesar Augustus or the glib-tongued denizens of Madison Avenue, feel that cruelty, horror, and sex should be treated lightly, coolly, as a joke. But the sick joke deserves—"deserves" is too strong a word; "requires" would be better—a chapter devoted to it alone. Its history and morphology are fascinating, repulsive but fascinating.

There are other forms of cruelty that cause comedy and laughter, but certainly we have mentioned enough forms to demonstrate that cruelty and comedy frequently have much in common. To point out that they have much in common is one thing, and an easy thing at that; to explain why they have much in common is not so easy. When we laugh at a scene of comic cruelty, we may be laughing in hysterical relief that we are not the victim. Certainly this theory has some merit. We all know about aesthetic distance; we all know that behind the footlights they make love in jest, they murder in jest, they beat in jest. We know, I say, because we are clever, we are sophisticated; but is everyone in on the secret? Constance Rourke tells of a remarkable incident in her brilliant work, *American Humor*. She is describing one member of an audience present at a performance of a melodrama in a Kentucky village. On the small stage a gambler's family was movingly portrayed as starving. This member of the audience, moved to compassion, rose and said, "I propose we make up something for this woman." Even after someone had whispered to him that it was all make-believe, he delivered a lecture on "the worthlessness of the gambler, flung a bill on the stage with his pocketbook, advised the woman not to let her husband know about it or he would spend it all on faro, and then with a divided mind sat down, saying, 'Now go on with the play.'"

Such naïveté is not confined to Kentucky backwoodsmen. George Burns described an event that happened to him in the Victoria Palace in London. He and Gracie Allen were playing to a packed house—but let him tell it:

> We had an encore that we used in case we were a hit. I would come out and say, "Ladies and Gentlemen, we would like to do a little more, but we're not prepared." Then Gracie would interrupt and say, "*I* am." Then she would talk, and then I would talk, until we were both talking competitively, and it would end with one of our big jokes.
>
> Opening night we were a hit and we were doing this encore. I said, "Ladies and Gentlemen, we would like to do a little more, but we're not prepared." Gracie said, "*I* am." She talked, I talked, we were both talking, and suddenly an English gentleman in white tie and tails who was sitting in the sixth row, and who apparently didn't understand it was part of the act, rose to his feet, snapped his fingers, and said, "See here, let the little lady carry on."

We may smile condescendingly as we hear the tale of the partly gullible, naïve, backwoodsman, or the tale of the supposedly sophisticated English gentleman, but certainly we have missed a great experience in life if we have not, at one time or another, felt such an identity with dramatic reality.

So we may laugh in relief that we are not the victims of the comic brutality, but I doubt that that is the only reason. Instead of being glad that we are not the victim, we may be identifying ourselves with the perpetrator of the cruelty. In that case, since we are humane and decent beings, the victim obviously deserves his comeuppance at our hands, and we are delighted that the ends of justice are being served. So that gives us another theory, also with some merit, that we like to see pomposity deflated, we like to see Sir Politic Would-Be in his tortoise shell, Malvolio in his dark room, Parolles blind-folded and bedevilled, and Sig Rumann, clad only in long underwear, locked in a closet.

While it is undoubtedly satisfying and laughable to see pomposity deflated, that, too, is only part of the answer. This theory, like the previous one, will not hold in all examples. We like to see comic antagonists and comic butts get what is coming to them, but how do we account for our laughter when the sympathetic comic character is beaten, gets incarcerated, or is subjected to other forms of the cruelly comic? We do laugh at the misadventures of Charlie Chaplin in the boxing ring, and in *City Lights* Chaplin is definitely a sympathetic comic character. And we do laugh at the discomfiture of Falstaff at Gadshill, and Falstaff is certainly a sympathetic comic character in 1 *Henry IV*. Bottom in *A Midsummer Night's Dream* is not a comic antagonist, but the sight of him in an ass's head is undoubtedly a source of laughter.

Our two theories, then, leave something to be desired. Each is valid some of the time; neither is valid all of the time; even if we combine them, we cannot justly claim that they will cover all the aspects of the cruelly comic. Perhaps, then, we may offer the theory that we laugh at cruelty if the pain that results from it is limited: it may hurt, but not maim; abuse, but not kill. Such discrimination requires tremendous objectivity on the part of the audience, but most audiences are able to be properly objective. Ashton Reid, writing on Buster Keaton, has this to say about timing and cruelty and comedy:

In the gag business, timing is the difference between a wow and a flop. Mr. Keaton learned this fact the hard way. When he was a mere stripling, part of the Three Keatons routine called for Old Man Keaton to whack Buster on the seat of the pants with a broom. The kid found out that if he yelled "Ouch!" instantly, no one laughed. If he ignored the whack, no one laughed. But if he ignored the whack for five seconds and then yelled—that was funny. It was funny because it conveyed the idea that it took five seconds for the whack to travel from Buster Keaton's pants seat to his brain.

Whether or not Reid's interpretation is correct, we have concrete evidence that audiences are able to discriminate—even five seconds worth. So we are unable to say that audiences are incapable of the necessary objectivity and discrimination. We are unable to say that insufficient time is available between the cruelty and the laugh. We cannot even fall back on the snide comment that far as we have progressed in twentieth-century physiology and psychology, no one as yet has invented a do-it-yourself pain-threshold detector. But there are examples to refute such a theory. Chaplin went beyond the limits mentioned above when he made death comic at least once in *Carmen*, occasionally in *The Great Dictator*, and many times in *Monsieur Verdoux*, which he had the courage to subtitle, "A comedy of murders." The animated cartoons featuring Popeye the Sailor deal in organized mayhem: bones are broken with finesse and casualness; arms and legs are stretched so freely that it seems as if a comic procrustean bed is controlling the action; necks are twisted round and round as if some dextrous hand were winding a clock. Tom Lehrer's songs treat death as comic on at least three occasions. Jonathan Swift's *Modest Proposal* deserves mention in this connection. In other words, there seem to be no limits to the extent and kind of cruelty that can cause laughter. None of the traditional theories seems to obtain when carefully examined. Surely there must be some reason why we laugh when we are presented with scenes of cruelty, brutality, and death. Perhaps we laugh because we know, consciously or unconsciously, that what we are watching is not real. I do not forget Constance Rourke's backwoodsman. He, too, in Miss Rourke's words, was of "divided mind." I do not forget George Burns's English gentleman, so fashionably attired in white tie and tails. The point of the Burns and Allen act was to convey the impression that what they were doing was spontaneous, unrehearsed, natural, not dramatic. The English gentleman can be excused if he saw fit to protest a blatant display of what he considered to be bad manners. It is easy, too easy, for us to forget that when we applaud at the final curtain of *Antony and Cleopatra*, we are applauding the representation of an action, not the action itself. We are not applauding the act of suicide; we are applauding the stage representation of the act. When we laugh at stage or screen representations of violence, cruelty, brutality, or death, we are probably laughing at the representations of the acts, not the acts themselves; when we laugh at practical jokes that really cause pain, we take time to gasp in horror. This time that we take, unconsciously to be sure, enables us to ascertain that the pain does not exceed the stated limits: hurt, but not maim; abuse, but not kill. Perhaps it is healthy that we do so. Perhaps by so doing we are able to purge ourselves of the latent sadism that is, to a greater or lesser measure, in all of us. This theory is, to be sure, Aristotelian, but only superficially so. In actuality it is, despite all of the nasty things that Plato had to say about comedy and the comic, Platonic. The representation of a cruel act on the stage is at least two, and probably three, removes from reality. If we actually think that the cruelty which we see enacted on the stage is real, we should not laugh, we should not applaud, we should take action. Because we know that it isn't real, we are enabled to dissolve in laughter. For we know full well that after the final curtain there will be no welts on the back, no bruises on the buttocks, no more ropes or chains confining arms and legs. And in the dressing room the stage corpse and his stage murderer will be sitting side by side as they remove their make-up. What are they discussing? Not, you may be sure, the Freudian theory of tendency wit, but a far more momentous problem: where will they go to have coffee and sandwiches?

*You taught me language, and my profit on't
Is I know how to curse.*

—Caliban in *The Tempest*

Cruelty and comedy (II): *"When you say* that, *frown!"*

A few years ago, the cruel joke, the sick joke, the Bloody Mary—it had many names—rapidly made its mephitic way across the country. Even now it has not completely disappeared. It has not died. Along with the sick comedian, it is merely hibernating in poorly lighted, badly ventilated caverns which are called "sophisticated supper clubs" by those in the know. Those in the know have also spent much time in high-level debate in an effort to ascertain the origin of the sick joke.

Most connoisseurs of the genre believe that its bloodline (I use the term advisedly) is simple: by Ivy League out of Madison Avenue. Some connoisseurs, however, are far more specific in their description: by Charles Addams out of Tom Lehrer.

> *"Mother, what's a vampire?"*
> *"Shut up, kid, and drink your blood."*

Whatever the bloodline, and some case can be made for each of the theories and many more in addition, by this time the country has definitely taken sides in a slightly less high-level debate to determine the sick joke's value. Those who approve of the sick joke feel that it provides a healthy, non-aggressive outlet for our latent sadistic impulses (I doubt that Freud would call the sick joke "non-aggressive") and, besides, it's funny. Those who disapprove feel that its flourishing gives more proof—if, indeed, more proof were needed—that delinquency of the juvenile, mature, and senile varieties is rampant (I somehow remember that Milton felt that no person had ever been corrupted by a book) and, besides, the sick joke is not amusing.

> *"Mother, why do I keep turning around in circles?"*
> *"Be quiet, Herbert, or I'll nail your other foot to the floor."*

Funny or not, healthy outlet or symptom of a moral illness, the sick joke flourished, particularly in the groves of academe and in the rarefied atmosphere where dwelt the entrepreneurs of the "communications" industry. Some people hoped that if they simply ignored it, it would go away. It didn't. It may have hibernated, but it did not disappear. It would seem that it is here for a while and, if we can't avoid it, and we can't, we had better try to understand it. I don't mean the joke itself, for the joke is obvious to the point of painfulness. I mean rather its source, its origin, for the two bloodlines given above are clearly superficial and interested far more in epigrammatic utterance than in truth. I mean, too, its reason for being in such a place as this, at such a time as now. These problems lead us, inevitably but unfortunately, into such forbidding areas as the history and sociology of literary taste. By a brief examination of literary history, we can see that the emotional attitude which creates the sick joke is a recurrent, not a unique, phenomenon; by gingerly dipping a tentative toe in the gelid waters of sociology, we may be able to see why it re-arose at precisely this time and in precisely this place.

"Something in a hearing aid, Mr. Van Gogh?"

The sick joke represents, it seems to me, an attempt to attain a superior, sophisticated attitude toward violence, sex, physical deformity, revealed religion, and death. In order to attain this attitude, the normal—one could almost say the "stock"—responses must appear to be ignored. We normally respond with horror to representations of violence. The sick joke asks us to laugh. We normally respond with a feeling of awe to representations of revealed religion. The sick joke asks us to snicker. We normally respond with compassion or sympathy when confronted with physical deformity. The sick joke wants us to be amused. But laughter, and snickers, and amusement are not enough. We must be aware as we laugh that what we are laughing at is not normally considered funny by those who are not so clever as we are. We must be aware that we are the initiated, the esoteric. We must feel superior, we must feel sophisticated in the presence of violence, sex, revealed religion, death, and physical deformity.

> *"Mrs. Jones, may Johnny come out and play baseball?"*
>
> *"Why, boys, how can you ask that? You know that Johnny is a quadruple amputee."*
>
> *"We know, but we need something for second base."*

It is easy to find examples through the ages of such sophistication. We can find it in some of the plays of Aristophanes, in many of the epigrams of Martial, in some of the *Meta-morphoses* and in sections of the *Ars Amatoria* of Ovid, in parts of the *Golden Ass* of Apuleius, in *Trimalchio's Dinner* by that *arbiter elegantiarum*, Petronius. I have by no means exhausted the classical period, but a few examples should suffice. The Middle Ages offer us some of the *Lais* of Marie de France, the sophisticated attitude toward illicit love of Chaucer's Pandarus and, indeed, of the entire courtly love tradition, the sophisticated attitude toward violence and the clergy of Chaucer's *fabliaux*, and the attitude toward physical deformity which is represented by the gargoyles on gothic cathedrals.

> *"Look, kid, I don't care who your father is—you don't walk on the water while I'm fishing."*

The Renaissance, even if we exclude some of the exquisite refinements on the art of torture developed by the Inquisition, gives us a rich lode to be mined. Just by confining ourselves to one literary figure, we have the youthful Shakespeare with his sophisticated attitude toward violence and death in *Titus Andronicus*, *Henry VI*, and *King John*; his sophisticated attitude toward violence, sex, physical deformity, religion, and death in *Richard III*; and his sophisticated attitude toward sex in *Venus and Adonis*. William T. Hastings has interpreted this attitude brilliantly in his excellent essay, "The Hardboiled Shakspere." Of *Venus and Adonis* he writes:

> At mention of "the boar" Venus nearly swoons,
> > "And on his neck her yoking arms she throws:
> > She sinketh down, still hanging by his neck,
> > He on her belly falls, she on her back."

There follow, as every schoolboy knows, some witty verses on the general subject of leading a horse to water. And then we pass to a dialogue between the two which rapidly develops into a debate on love, lust, and "increase." The more innocent of modern readers may forget the pose of the two debaters . . . but we can be sure that for Shakespeare and his courtly readers therein lay the special savor of the passage, than which it would be difficult to imagine anything more hardboiled.

Only the more innocent of modern readers will forget the pose of the two debaters. Hastings has caught in essence the attitude that I am trying to describe. He may call this attitude hardboiled, and I may call it sophisticated, but there is basically no difference between the two attitudes. I suppose it is unnecessary to mention either to the hardboiled reader or to the sophisticated reader that this debate episode in *Venus and Adonis* lasts from line 592 to line 810 of the poem, 219 lines of what might well be called sophisticated titillation.

> *"Mother, may I have a new dress for Easter?"*
> *"No, you may not, Edward."*

After the time of Shakespeare, there are the scenes of horror with which the Jacobean dramatists sought to thrill and titillate their audiences, and the smart, superior, clever, even smutty, attitudes toward love, lust, and sex which Vanbrugh and Wycherley imposed upon the audiences of the Restoration. Then there was the eighteenth century, the Age of Reason, the Age of Wit, the age of Pope and the *Dunciad*, and Swift and his scatalogical poetry. And before we leave the eighteenth century, surely we have time to mention the super-sophistication of John Cleland's attitude. According to report, Cleland, finding himself without funds, sought to rectify his impecunious situation. Unemployment insurance was unknown in the eighteenth century. He therefore set out to write a book that would be as lewd as possible. He also set for himself—so the tradition runs—an almost impossible restriction: he would use no word which could possibly offend the most proper of men and women. The result, successful if you consider his original intention, was his notorious book, *Fanny Hill, or The Memoirs of a Woman of Pleasure*. It is true that no individual word offends, but the book is indisputably salacious. How sophisticated can you get?

> *"Tell me, Jocasta, what was that difficulty you had with your second husband?"*

Then, still in the eighteenth century but lapping over into the nineteenth, and just across the English Channel, there was Count Donatien Alphonse François Sade, better known as the Marquis de Sade. He gave three words, "sadism," "sadist," and "sadistic" to the dictionaries, and thousands of pages in which cruelty and violence and lewdness are inextricably united, to the world. His leading characters, both male and female, are always aware, intellectually aware, of what they are doing and why they are doing it. They are not immoral but amoral. They never lose themselves in complete emotional abandon as other, more normal, mortals do. Simone de Beauvoir, in her perceptive essay, "Must We Burn Sade?" describes with insight and accuracy the attitude of the Sade protagonist:

> The male aggression of the Sadist Hero is never softened by the usual transformation of the body into flesh. He never, for an instant, loses himself in his animal nature; he remains so lucid, so cerebral, that philosophic discourse, far from dampening his ardor, acts as an aphrodisiac.

Mlle de Beauvoir is undoubtedly correct in her description and in her analysis. The effect of Sade's books on the reader is something else again: Sade's philosophical discourse acts not as an aphrodisiac, but as a soporific; his description of sex and violence act not as an aphrodisiac, but as an emetic.

And the same may be said of the books of Leopold von Sacher-Masoch. He, like Sade, gave three words, "masochism," "masochist," and "masochistic" to the dictionaries, but he gave, fortunately, far fewer pages and far less philosophical utterance to the world. As a matter of fact, it is doubtful that Sacher-Masoch belongs in Sade's company at all. He is far less cerebral, imaginative, and vicious than his notorious predecessor. It is customary to link the two, explaining blandly that, after all, masochism is merely the reverse of the coin of which sadism is the obverse. While there may be some degree of merit in this linking, there is, I feel, a fundamental difference implicit in these perversions. Sade's hero makes every effort to insure that his victim has no possibility of pleasure. He generally rationalizes his behavior by maintaining that if the victim derives any pleasure, the hero's pleasure is reduced by just that much. To consider pleasure in such a light seems extremely cold-blooded and dispassionate. Yet it must be remembered that the Sade hero is cerebral above all. Such calculation is part of his reason for being. Sacher-Masoch's victim-protagonist seems to take the diametrically opposite point of view: the more pleasure the tormentor gets, the more the victim-protagonist's pleasure is increased. In short, the masochist needs a morbidly cruel person for a tormentor; the sadist is far more self-sufficient in that he needs only an object, not a personality. I may be totally wrong in this judgment, but I find it hard to believe that a victim of physical cruelty is able to rise above his situation as easily as an inflictor of physical cruelty. The sadist hero, completely dominating his situation, can and does easily deprive his victim of any prospect of pleasure; the masochistic hero, completely dominated by his situation, neither has nor desires such control over his tormentor. Sade is, then, more intellectual; Sacher-Masoch is more physical and emotional. Both writers, however, demonstrate a sophisticated attitude toward violence, cruelty, religion, sex, and horror.

"*Why don't you try Carter's Little Liver Pills, Mr. Prometheus?*"

When we reach Sacher-Masoch's algolagnia in our investigation of the cerebral attitude toward violence and sex, we have gone, briefly and superficially, from classical Greece to the end of the nineteenth century. Certainly this survey is not exhaustive. The works could be and should be analyzed more closely. We could range far more widely in time and space and not come to the end of such a survey. Certainly some time could be given to the tales of Boccaccio told by the gentle folk of Florence who fled the plague; certainly some mention could be made of the paintings of Lucas Cranach the Elder or the etchings of Albrecht Dürer; I miss, too, some discussion of the gigantic laughter of Rabelais, the horror of Swift, the perversions of Swinburne and Wilde, the childish cruelty of *Mother Goose* and *Alice in Wonderland*. But we are now in the twentieth century. Along with the thermonuclear bomb, the twentieth century has given birth to the sick joke, and we must examine, again briefly, the twentieth-century literary sources and analogues of this phenomenon.

> *"Mother, why is daddy so cold, so white, and so pale?"*
> *"Shut up, Herbert, and dig."*

The twentieth century is replete with sources and analogues of the sick joke, with examples of the sophisticated attitude that we've been discussing. The problem is not finding the examples, but selecting from the myriads that are available. We find them in the writings of two of our Nobel prize winners, Hemingway and Faulkner. The Faulkner of *Sanctuary* certainly had a cool, sophisticated attitude toward violence and sex. Certainly, too, if you consider *Sanctuary* an unfair example because it is, admittedly, an early work and a potboiler, Faulkner maintains this attitude (not, to be sure, to the exclusion of other attitudes) in his saga of the Sutpen clan, several volumes of which have won critical acclaim, in several of his most brilliant short stories, and in the tales of the house of Snopes. And the Hemingway of "The Killers" had this attitude, too. Note the cool, purely objective, completely dispassionate attitude toward death in this passage:

> "What are you going to kill Ole Andreson for? What did he ever do to you?"
> "He never had a chance to do anything to us. He never even seen us."

"And he's only going to see us once," Al said from the kitchen.

"What are you going to kill him for, then?" George asked.

"We're killing him for a friend. Just to oblige a friend, bright boy."

"The Killers" was written about 1927, and Hemingway was young. He was still young, but it was some ten years later, when he wrote *To Have And Have Not*. There are some healthy, normal attitudes toward sex and violence in the book, but there is an awareness of the sophisticated attitudes, too. Here is Helen Gordon as she talks to the husband she is about to leave:

"Everything I believed in and everything I cared about I left for you because you were so wonderful and you loved me so much that love was all that mattered. Love was the greatest thing wasn't it? Love was what we had that no one else had or could ever have? And you were a genius and I was your whole life. I was your partner and your little black flower. Slop. Love is just another dirty lie. Love is ergoapiol pills to make me come around because you were afraid to have a baby. Love is quinine and quinine and quinine until I'm deaf with it. Love is that dirty aborting horror that you took me to. Love is my insides all messed up. It's half catheters and half whirling douches. I know about love. Love always hangs up behind the bathroom door. It smells like lysol. To hell with love."

Then thirty years after "The Killers," and twenty years after *To Have And Have Not*, in the Centennial Issue of *The Atlantic Monthly* which appeared in November, 1957, Hemingway had a short story entitled "A Man of the World." In the story there is a description of a knock-down-and-drag-out fight between two men. One of the men has gouged out the eyeball of his opponent. The vile jelly is hanging down on the victim's cheek when a spectator offers some cool, dispassionate advice: "Bite it off! Bite it off just like it was a grape." Such attitudes toward violence are not confined to men in Hemingway's writings. Mrs. Macomber's thoughts and actions in the denouement of "The Short Happy Life of Francis Macomber" provide ample proof that the female of the species is at least as deadly as the male.

We might notice also some other writers, not Nobel prize winners. In Dashiell Hammett's short stories (particularly the conclusions of "The Gutting of Couffignal" and "The Girl with the Silver Eyes"), in his novel *Red Harvest*, and in his novelette *Nightmare Town*, violence and death are as common as eating. There are sophisticated attitudes toward love and sex in his novels *The Thin Man* and *The Maltese Falcon*. Sophisticated attitudes towards sex and religion abound in James M. Cain's *Serenade*, and sophisticated attitudes toward sex and violence are certainly present in his *Double Indemnity*. About 40,000,000 copies of Mickey Spillane's detective novels have been sold. Rarely in them does anyone die a natural death, or does anyone get knocked out by a clean punch in the jaw, or is there a normal sexual relationship. Women in Spillane's novels die by having their navels tattooed by .45 caliber slugs, or by having their hair set on fire. Men are knocked unconscious by having their teeth hammered down their throats. Love affairs in Spillane's novels deal more with the whip than with the caress, more with the bite than with the kiss. So far as Ian Fleming is concerned, his James Bond is merely a smoother, better educated, trade-name-dropping Mike Hammer.

Nor are these attitudes in the twentieth century confined to literature. We have Dali and Picasso in painting, Randall Thompson and Stravinsky in music, Addams and Virgil Partch in cartooning. The Hollywood myth-makers exploited these attitudes in *Scarface*, *Little Caesar*, and *Public Enemy*. On second thought, such motion pictures seem, in the sixties, peculiarly restrained. After all, the thirties are many years away, and we have *The Tingler* now. We've come a long distance, if you don't care what you say, since we got a thrill out of watching James Cagney shove a grapefruit into the delicate features of Mae Clarke in *Public Enemy*.

"*Aside from that, Mrs. Lincoln, how did you enjoy the play?*"

So, while the attitudes that produce the sick joke in the twentieth century have always been with us in one form or another, they seem to have reached a peak in our time. Perhaps people of today are more conscious of, more concerned with, their motives than ever before. Violence and death and horror and sex and religion have always been known to men, despite all the talk of a golden age; and some men have always taken a hardboiled, sophisticated, dispassionate, calculating attitude toward them. Certainly the man of the twentieth century has had every opportunity to become hardened to violence and death and horror. Three wars in forty years, nuclear fission and nuclear fusion, space satellites, intercontinental ballistic missiles, and lunar probes have all combined to force man to create a shell around his more tender and gentle emotions. Frightened in the past, uneasy in the present, terrified of the future, man in the twentieth century first turned for surcease to the sentimental drivel of cheap fiction, then to the facile emotional happy endings of some motion pictures and some television dramas. These trifled with his emotions, cheaply, glibly, easily. He needed an antidote. Perhaps that is why we have had the sick joke in such a time as now, in such a place as here.

Let us grant it is not
Amiss to tumble on the bed of Ptolemy
To give a kingdom for a mirth . . .
— Octavius Caesar in *Antony and Cleopatra*

Love, sex, and comedy

If it is true, as Compton Mackenzie and David Daiches have suggested, that *stupid* is the only word in English that rhymes with *Cupid*, it is little wonder that creators of comedy, who generally have excellent ears for a rhyme as well as for a pun, have often looked to love and sex as sources of comedy and laughter. Certainly, the behavior of people in love or in heat has long been considered comic by objective observers. *Objective observers* may, in this case, be defined as people possessed of the genuine comic spirit who are not, at the moment, in love or in heat themselves. The English-speaking peoples, despite their unique rhyme, are not alone in considering love and sex a source of the comic. Homer and Aristophanes, Plautus and Ovid, Boccaccio and Marie de France, Machiavelli and Cervantes, Molière and Jean Giraudoux—the list could be infinitely extended—all testify to the laughter inherent in love and in sex. The laughter may be as gentle as that of Cervantes, as vicious and sneering as that of Machiavelli, may be the result of a Plautine bludgeon, or of a Giraudoux rapier, but it exists inevitably, universally, in every age, culture, and language.

Meredith would probably issue a caveat here, insisting that a society of cultivated men and particularly women is essential before you can have creators of the comic who will find comedy in love and in sex. He would go further and insist that you must have a society that treats women with equality before such a condition obtains. But for Meredith, only one type of comedy really exists, the comedy of manners. And the comedy of manners insists not on the equality of women but on their superiority. That is why Meredith likes Molière, whose Celimène, for example, is far superior to his Alceste; why he likes Congreve, whose Millamant is far superior (except in one key scene) to his Mirabell; why he sees to it in his own novel that Clara Middleton triumphs over Sir Willoughby Patterne. Because of their treatment of women, he does not feel that the Arabs can have great comedy (he thinks that *The One Thousand and One Nights* is grossly, not delicately, comic). For the same reason, he does not think that the Italians can have great comedy (he knows of Machiavelli and Goldoni, but he never seems to mention the *Commedia dell' Arte*). Also for the same reason, and despite Goethe, and Heine, and Jean Paul Richter, he thinks that the Germans are sadly deficient in comedy (he never mentions

Tyl Eulenspiegel and, unfortunately, he never had the opportunity to know of Marlene Dietrich, whom C. H. Rand has described so well:

I want a woman whose passion is not a blind rage of the body or the soul, but a recognition of mutual attraction in which reason or humour will play their part, as far as love permits. But vamps with brains are far to seek. And vamps with humour even further. I find all my requisites in the screen character of Marlene Dietrich. She has beauty in abundance. She has a rich, sensuous allure. And you only have to look at her eyes to see that she has brains, and at her mouth to see that she has humour.

Certainly Meredith would accept this description (with the possible exception of the phrase "as far as love permits") as a definition of the ideal heroine of the ideal comedy of manners. And if it be argued that here has been described a woman, not a character, I should point out that anyone who has seen Miss Dietrich as Lola Lola in *Der Blaue Engel,* or as Amy Jolly in *Morocco,* or as Shanghai Lily in *Shanghai Express,* or as Madeline in *Desire,* or even in her bit part as the denizen of the Barbary Coast saloon in Mike Todd's *Around the World in Eighty Days,* would find it difficult, if not impossible, to determine where the woman leaves off and the character begins. And this character, this woman, has wit, humor, and a healthy sense of the comic along with the frank invitation to love and even to sex that her appearance and her voice extend. Miss Dietrich's appeal is so great that even Carol Channing's brilliantly devastating impersonation of her reminds us not of her stylistic excesses but only that it has been too long since we last saw Marlene perform. Even if Maria Magdalene Dietrich were merely the creation and Josef von Sternberg were the creator—which I do not for a moment believe—and even if there were no high comedy in Goethe, in Heine, in Jean Paul Richter—which I do not for a moment believe— then the nation which produced Josef von Sternberg and Bertolt Brecht and the Thomas Mann of *Felix Krull* has learned it well. Along with the *weltschmerz* there is now high comedy, along with the *gemütlichkeit* there is now wit.

Love and sex have been made comic by the understatement of high comedy, by the understatement of wit, but they can be made comic too by overstatement. Certainly the overstatement of the moans and groans of despair caused by unrequited love can be comic to the observer, no matter how pathetic the groans may be to the victim. In *As You Like It* Rosalind, disguised as a young man, has promised to cure the love-sick Orlando. After all, he needs curing. Jaques complains that he has been marring trees by writing love songs in their bark. As he hangs one of his poems on a tree, he bellows forth in high, astounding terms the undeviating, one-track mind of the man overcome by love sickness:

> Hang there, my verse, in witness of my love;
>   And thou, thrice-crowned Queen of Night, survey
> With thy chaste eye, from thy pale sphere above,
>   The huntress' name that my full life doth sway.
> O Rosalind! these trees shall be my books,
>   And in their barks my thoughts I'll character
> That every eye which in this forest looks
>   Shall see thy virtue witness'd everywhere.
> Run, run, Orlando! carve on every tree
> The fair, the chaste, and unexpressive she.

Her cure, she says, will be a relatively simple one, one that she used before in a similar case:

> He was to imagine me his love, his mistress; and I set him every day to woo me. At which time would I, being but a moonish youth, grieve, be effeminate, changeable, longing, and liking, proud, fantastical, apish, shallow, inconstant, full of tears, full of smiles; for every passion something, and for no passion truly anything, as boys and women are for the most part cattle of this colour; would now like him, now loathe him; then entertain him, then forswear him; now weep for him, then spit at him. . . .

Merely the description of the remedy, a shrewd analysis of the behavior of the fickle and changeable female, should effect a cure, but Orlando is sure that the cure won't work in his case. He is, though, willing to try. He arrives for the first installment of his cure an hour late. He is rated for that. Some more shrewish dialogue follows and then Rosalind announces: "Well, in her person, I say I will not have you." Orlando replies: "Then in mine own person, I die." Rosalind's answer to Orlando's bromide about dying for love is a classic rejoinder to all lovesick idiots, all who overstate the pangs of despised love:

No, faith, die by attorney. The poor world is almost six thousand years old, and in all this time there was not any man died in his own person, videlicet, in a love cause. Troilus had his brains dash'd out with a Grecian club; yet he did what he could to die before, and he is one of the patterns of love. Leander, he would have liv'd many a fair year though Hero had turn'd nun, if it had not been for a hot midsummer night; for (good youth) he went but forth to wash him in the Hellespont, and being taken with the cramp, was drown'd; and the foolish chroniclers of that age found it was "Hero of Sestos." But these are all lies. Men have died from time to time, and worms have eaten them, but not for love.

The sensible humor of Rosalind's answer serves to puncture the laughable pretension of all those who claim that they will die for love. What is the comic answer to the pretensions of those who claim that their love is as deep as the ocean, that it will last for all eternity? Many answers can be and have been given. Even some lines taken out of context would provide answers. "The lady [or gentleman, as the case may be] doth protest too much, methinks." "They build no temples to the rising of the sun who howl not in terror when the dragon eats the sun." Rosalind again provides a good answer. She has asked Orlando how long he would have his love after he has possessed her, and he has answered, "For ever and a day." Her reply cuts the protestation down to size: "Say 'a day' without the 'ever.'"

Make no mistake. A woman in love speaks this line, but Rosalind knows that being in love does not mean being devoid of reason, does not mean that you are blinded to the ways of the world. When you do get blinded to the ways of the world, you tend to use overstatement of idea, even though your previous training has schooled you in a terse, cryptic, prose style:

> CLEOPATRA: If it be love indeed, tell me how much.
> ANTONY: There's beggary in the love that can be reckon'd.
> CLEOPATRA: I'll set a bourne how far to be belov'd.
> ANTONY: Then must thou needs find out new heaven, new earth.

Tragedy, not comedy, results from this colloquy at the beginning of *Antony and Cleopatra*, but you do not have to consider Antony transformed into a strumpet's fool to regard his lines as mildly amusing. Shakespeare has set the lines brilliantly in context. The play opens with Philo's savage commentary on the decline of Antony from a great general to a mere lover. At that point, Antony, Cleopatra, and their retinue enter, and the lovers speak the lines cited above. A messenger then enters with news from Rome. Antony is annoyed at the intrusion and merely wants to hear the headlines, not the full account. Cleopatra takes this opportunity to tease Antony, to provoke him, to irritate him—the slang term "needle" is really the right word in this context. She is successful. He spouts more phrases of love and dismisses the messenger without hearing his news: "Speak not to us." The triple pillar of the world has been transformed and, at this early stage of the play, we are forced to laugh at his overstatement in idea and deed of how much he loves her. Philo has been proved right, and the sight and sound of this great warrior made a babbling lover by the seductive Cleopatra stimulate our laughter, even though his death will later stimulate our tears.

Perhaps the comic epitaph for all those who moan about love and for all those who overstate their love is given by Mercutio in *Romeo and Juliet*. He has been complaining to

Benvolio about how love has ruined Romeo, when Romeo appears on the scene. Mercutio starts a wit combat with him and Romeo answers with as good as he receives. Mercutio is happy to see Romeo once more in a delightful, witty mood, and proclaims his happiness in brilliantly comic, though mildly obscene, terms:

Why, is this not better now than groaning for love? Now art thou sociable, now art thou Romeo; now art thou what thou art, by art as well as nature. For this drivelling love is like a great natural that runs lolling up and down to hide his bauble in a hole.

The comic overstatement of the love situation is not confined to moans and words. Despite the preoccupation of the contemporary American male with what S. J. Perelman has called *la haute poitrine*, physical endowment can be overstated, too, and the result of the overstatement can be comic. Marie Wilson is a case in point, Dagmar is a case in point, Diana Dors, Jayne Mansfield, and Marilyn Monroe are cases in point. But all of these actresses, even Miss Monroe whose comic range was far greater than that of the others, owe a tremendous debt to Mae West. Miss West actually lacked the physical charms of some of these younger women, but she gave the appearance of possessing more than they. She acted her roles with such a light-hearted vulgarity and such a surface sexuality that the result, despite the reformers, was not obscenity but comedy. In addition to her other, more obvious assets, her voice and delivery made her a magnificent comedienne. She could make the most innocuous, the most obvious, remark sound almost sinister; but then the toss of the head, the shrug of the shoulders, the slouch in her walk that accompanied the words would turn the words from the frankly sexual to the delightfully laughable. For the sake of an example, consider just one of her films. In *She Done Him Wrong* (1933) she plays the role of Lou, the Queen of the Bowery in the nineties. Her songs are those that we'd expect of her:

"Frankie and Johnny," "Easy Rider," and "I Like a Man Who Takes His Time." Sexuality, even obscenity, are present in all three, but the overstatement of voice and delivery make them hilariously comic. Her lines, too, are what we would expect of her. "Lady Lou," says one character, "You're a fine woman." Her answer, despite the *double entendre*, gets to the heart of the matter: "A finer woman never walked the streets." She can be wryly philosophical about the double standard: "When women go wrong, men go right after them." She can use a quip to cover the fact that she's too busy thinking of another's welfare to have much concern for herself: "Your bath is ready, Miss Lou." "You take it. I'm indisposed." Surely the line, "Why don't you come up some time—and see me?" seems on the surface to be fairly innocent, but the voice, the delivery, the rising emphasis on the word "up," the upward flick of the eyes, take the line from the innocent, through the frankly sensual, to the comic. She can be completely and thoroughly matter of fact as she says, "Diamonds is my career." Then there is one line in the film that demonstrates completely that her lively sense of the ridiculous can puncture more economically than Rosalind, if not so brilliantly, the fatuousness of the dying-swan type of lover. A suitor full of hoarse sincerity says to her, "I'd die to make you happy." She merely flicks him with her patented look as she says, with great comic sensuality, "You wouldn't be any good to me then." Economical and pointed utterance is always her specialty, and she manages to dispose both of men and of the institution of marriage in one pithy statement: "He'd be the kind a gal would have to marry to get rid of."

Some of her lines are amusing even when baldly set down on paper, but when the tone of voice is recalled, when the sensuous walk is recalled, when the not particularly attractive but definitely overblown figure is recalled, the amusing is changed to the hilarious, the smile is changed to the belly laugh. The censors thought that she should be censored, and saw to it that she was. They made, as they almost always do, a serious mistake. Her appeal was always to the comic, not to the prurient, interest, to the funny bone, not to the genitalia.

I have heard it argued that Miss West's suggestive walk and suggestive talk and suggestive leer were far worse than the frank filth of the burlesque house. I have never been completely sure just what the other term of the comparison was. A lot of things happened on the stage of the burlesque house, whether the house was Minsky's in New York, or the Modern in Providence, R. I., or the Old Howard (known as the "Atheneum" to the esoteric) in Boston. There was strip teasing, to be sure, but there was also the tenor or the lyric soprano, there were the many chorus numbers, there was the brilliant spiel of the candy butcher during the intermissions as he sold candy, ice cream, soft drinks, and other, less savory, merchandise, and, above all, there were the comic routines. I say "above all" because I actually believe that some people went to burlesque theaters for the comedians, not for the "30 beautiful girls 30." That such people were in the minority, I agree; that they were the true connoisseurs of burlesque, I insist. They were far greater connoisseurs, for example, than the intense but narrow-visioned friend of mine who used to arrive at the burlesque house just before the intermission, sit through the candy butcher's spiel, and leave before the second-act curtain rose; and far greater connoisseurs than another friend of mine, a professor of English, who used to maintain, with just the hint of a raised eyebrow, that he attended burlesque shows because the audience there was as close to the Elizabethan audience as it is possible to get in the twentieth century. But even the connoisseurs stopped going to burlesque shows because the quality of humor started to decline. And the great comic performers both male and female who could have stemmed the tide, those performers who didn't find it necessary to base every joke on incipient or overt homosexuality, were lured away by the legitimate theater, by the productions of Ziegfield or Earl Carroll, by the motion pictures, by the radio and television networks, by the nightclubs of New York, Miami, and Las Vegas.

Of course the reformers and the censors thought that burlesque should be prevented from despoiling the American cultural landscape, and with burlesque as with Miss West they were successful. And again they were wrong. For most often the burlesque show, by definition and by fact, appealed to the comic, not to the prurient, interest. It was difficult to take Rose La Rose seriously after Mike Sacks had introduced her as "the glamorous, glorious, glandular flower who sheds her petals—red hot Rose La Rose!" It was difficult to look seriously at any strip teaser when your eyes were still blurred with tears of laughter after watching the antics of Phil Silvers or Mike Sacks or Bobbie Clark, those great top bananas. In the twenties and thirties Gypsy Rose Lee was the darling of the intellectuals. She couldn't sing very well; her dancing was even worse than her singing; she wasn't particularly beautiful; but she was literate, she was bizarre, and she had a lively sense of the ridiculous. Everyone knows Gypsy the strip teaser, the author, the raconteur, and Gypsy knows herself:

H. L. Mencken called me an ecdysiast. I have also been described as deciduous. [Compare Mike Sacks and Rose La Rose above.] The French call me a deshabilleuse. In less-refined circles I'm known as a strip teaser.

Ashton Stevens overstated the case, but only slightly, when he said that she was "the only member of the cuticle sisterhood who can make nudity witty." Others had this ability, too, though after you mention Gypsy and Georgia Sothern and Lily St. Cyr and Ann Corio the names come hard. When all is considered, I still think that Mae West's walk, talk, and leer were suggestive, to be sure, but suggestive more of comedy than of sex. And I still believe that the great performers in burlesque both thought and acted as if comedy were burlesque's end product, and the display of physical charms were merely the means to that end.

For when sex is not amusing it can, at its best, lead to tragedy, but unfortunately it leads most often to melodrama and soap opera. Marya Mannes, a woman of wit and perception, has seen the problem and has stated it clearly. In a volume of essays entitled *More In Anger*, she has written a little fantasy in play form called "The Magic Box." The time is A.D. 2000. The place is a heath, blasted. The characters are A Very Old Man and A Student. "The *student* is making notes on what looks like papyrus with what looks like a stylus." The Very Old Man is trying to explain to The Student what television was like in America in the 1950's. Eventually The Very Old Man gets to soap operas, and the following dialogue ensues:

OLD MAN: There was, too, I remember, an extraordinary form of drama called the soap opera . . .

STUDENT: Soap opera?

OLD MAN: Yes. Because the makers of soap paid for them, not because they had music. Many million women watched them every day, and wept.

STUDENT: Wept? Why?

OLD MAN: Because their troubles were slight compared to those of the characters, who lived from calamity to calamity; and they wept from relief.

STUDENT: But what were these dramas about?

OLD MAN: They were about very stupid people who were either good or bad. But they were good and bad in very special ways . . .

STUDENT: What ways, old man?

OLD MAN: Well, all good women did housework all day and drank coffee. All bad women had careers, flirted with men, and drank cocktails.

STUDENT: And the men?

OLD MAN: I seem to remember that the bad men were usually cultivated, witty, and upper-class; and all the good men were dull, faithful, and humorless. You see, in America there was nothing funny about love, or sex. It was either nobly matrimonial, ignobly adulterous, or painfully adolescent. But it was never amusing.

STUDENT: Poor Americans!

Poor Americans, indeed. The young man is not wasting his compassion, if what this Aristotelian old man says is true. And, so far as soap operas were and are concerned, the old man is speaking the truth. His speech, however, does not confine itself to the soap opera. He says quite bluntly, ". . . in America there was nothing funny about love or sex. . . . it was never amusing." But Miss Mannes is obviously exaggerating for effect. She knows as well as anyone—and better than most—that Americans have been able to laugh at love and sex. Merely a short time intervened between Theda Bara's role of The Vamp in *A Fool There Was* (1914) and Marie Dressler's parody of the role in one episode of *Tillie's Punctured Romance* (1914). Rudolph Valentino's asthmatic love making in *The Sheik* (1921) was satirized by Ben Turpin's *The Shriek of Araby* (1923). Valentino's *Blood and Sand* (1922) was satirized by Stan Laurel's *Mud and Sand* in the same year. Elinor Glyn's heady Ruritanian romance, *Three Weeks*, starring Aileen Pringle and Conrad Nagel (1924), was satirized in a matter of months by Madeline Hurlock and Ben Turpin in *Three and a Half Weeks* (1924).

Eventually, even the feature film began to show that love and sex can be portrayed in an amusing manner, and we were blessed with such productions as *It Happened One Night*, starring Clark Gable and Claudette Colbert, and *The Thin Man* with William Powell, Myrna Loy, and a dog named Asta. These two films, both produced in 1934, started a vogue that is, despite Miss Mannes' comment, fortunately still going on. The late thirties saw such films as *Bringing up Baby*, in which Cary Grant and Katharine Hepburn were portrayed as cultivated, witty, and upper-class; *Destry Rides Again*, in which neither James Stewart nor Marlene Dietrich was upper class or cultivated, but in which both were witty; and *Ninotchka,* a film in which even Greta Garbo laughed. The forties were, perhaps properly, concerned with the war and its aftermath, but there was still a demand for *The Road to Morocco* and the other "Road" films, starring Bing Crosby, Bob Hope, and Dorothy Lamour; still a demand for such a film as *The Miracle of Morgan's Creek* with Betty Hutton, William Demarest, and Eddie Bracken, in which a young girl's pregnancy was the source of much of the laughter; still a demand for such a film as *To Have and Have Not,* in which Humphrey Bogart, Hoagy Carmichael, and Lauren Bacall made us forget, if only for a moment, that the motion picture had nothing in common with the Hemingway novel, that it had no plot worth mentioning, and that the diction of the hard-boiled school can be as formalized as a page out of Doctor Johnson. In speaking of Miss Bacall's performance in this film, James Agee gets to the root of the problem of love, sex, and comedy. He says:

[It] is a leisurely series of mating duels between Humphrey Bogart at his most proficient and the very entertaining, nervy, adolescent new blonde, Lauren Bacall. Whether or not you like the film will depend I believe on whether you like Miss Bacall. I am no judge. I can hardly look at her, much less listen to her—she has a voice like a chorus by Kid Ory—without getting caught in a dilemma between a low whistle and a bellylaugh.

Agee's review was written in 1944, but both his opinion and the motion picture still stand up today. And perhaps because of these films of the thirties and forties, we are able to enjoy light-hearted, amusing treatments of love and sex in such films of the fifties and early sixties as *The Seven Year Itch, The French Line, To Catch a Thief, The Prince and the Showgirl, Some Like It Hot* (even though I have a personal aversion to transvestitism), *Pillow Talk, Once More with Feeling,* and *The Apartment.*

I could include many plays, novels, and short stories that

obviously belong in this genre, but I have confined myself to films for one reason: Marya Mannes' Old Man was speaking from a background of televised soap opera when he made his comment about love never being amusing in America. I thought it only fair to disprove his statement by reference to a medium that is hedged in with as many restrictions as television, if not more.

Much of what I have been saying here has been concerned with America and the twentieth century. While love and sex have been treated amusingly in this country and in this time, one aspect of love and sex—an aspect which has been considered the apotheosis of the sexually comic in many cultures and in many ages—has rarely been considered a proper subject for comedy in our time and place. I refer, of course, to the cuckold and cuckoldry. Americans, if we are to judge from their literature, consider the cuckold a melodramatic or a tragic, rather than a comic, figure. They do not consider cuckoldry a laughing matter. If we don't mind perverting Shakespeare's meaning slightly, we could sum up the American attitude by quoting the refrain lines of one of the songs in *As You Like It*:

> Take thou no scorn to wear the horn;
> It was a crest ere thou wast born:
>   Thy father's father wore it,
>   And thy father bore it.
> The horn, the horn, the lusty horn,
> Is not a thing to laugh to scorn.

It is difficult to ascertain why there is no American *Mandragola*, or American *Country Wife*, or even an American *Baker's Wife*. You might argue that laughter is a talisman, an amulet, a charm that the average man uses as a sort of mystical defense against the operation of customs which he hates, but which he is unable to overcome. You could go further and argue that since the operation of these customs is inevitable, the average man uses laughter as a before-the-fact or after-the-fact antidote. Such a custom might be the law of the first night or the right of the lord. Americans, in general, have not known the custom. You could argue in another direction and maintain that marriage is a legal or an ecclesiastical, but not an emotional, bond. Outwitting the law, since the law is an ass, could be the cause of laughter. Such an argument might be maintained among a people who had such a custom as the marriage of convenience. Americans, in general, have not known such a custom. There are, undoubtedly, other reasons, sociological, psychological, economic, why Americans, according to their literature, do not laugh at cuckoldry, but the fact remains that in American literature the cuckold becomes a tragic or even a compassionate figure. For proof, one need only go to one month in the year 1924. In November of that year two plays appeared: Eugene O'Neill's *Desire Under the Elms* and Sidney Howard's *They Knew What They Wanted*. In each play, an old farmer becomes a cuckold. O'Neill's farmer, cuckolded by his son, is a tragic figure in his madness; Howard's farmer, cuckolded by his hired man, may be a comic figure to some but surely will be regarded as a tender and compassionate figure by most. Tony Patucci is no saint. He has his moment of madness when he finds that the child his wife Amy is bearing is not his, but he recovers his sanity and makes it clear that emotion is more important than intellect, more important than law:

TONY: . . . I want dis baby, Amy. Joe don' want him. Ees Tony want him. Amy, . . . Amy, . . . For God's sake don' go away an' leave Tony!

AMY: But, Tony! Think of what I have done?

TONY: What you done was mistake in da head, not in da heart. . . . Mistake in da head is no matter.

Because Tony is able to convince Amy that a mistake in the head doesn't matter, *They Knew What They Wanted*, is, I suppose, a comedy. It has, at least, a happy ending. And so does Frank Loesser's musical version of the same play. The cuckold in *Most Happy Fella* and *They Knew What They Wanted* is not an object of scorn. Because he has understanding, he is understood. Because he has compassion and sympathy for the girl who has erred, we have compassion and sympathy for him.

The contrast between Tony Patucci and Messer Nicia in Machiavelli's *Mandragola* is instructive in this connection. Messer Nicia, a dirty old man who'd make a cat laugh, literally forces his wife to cuckold him. Of course he is tricked into doing so, but we do not sympathize with him when he is tricked. How can we? He is perfectly willing to sacrifice the life of another and his wife's virtue so that his foolish desires may be fulfilled. His frenzied attempts to persuade his wife, Lucrezia, to go along with his plan increase our laughter. He suborns Lucrezia's confessor, Fra Timoteo; he convinces Sostrata, Lucrezia's mother, that she ought to aid in the plan; he takes part in a "kidnaping" of an "innocent" young man that will, he believes, result in that young man's death. He does all these things without compunction, without qualm. We are delighted that he is cuckolded. We are delighted that this avaricious old man pays for the doubtful privilege. We are even more delighted to learn that the cuckoldry will continue. Callimaco, the young Florentine who had conceived the entire plan because of his love for Lucrezia, talks after the fact to Ligurio, the parasite. He fills us in on all the details including—what is most important to us—Lucrezia's state of mind:

As I told you, Ligurio, till after one o'clock I wasn't really happy about it, and though my pleasure was great, I was not able to enjoy it. But after I had told her who I was, and had made her understand how much I loved her, and how easily we could live happily without it involving any scandal, thanks to the foolishness of her husband, and had promised that when God had other plans for him I would marry her at once—and when on top of all this she had felt the difference between my love and Messer Nicia's, and between the kisses of a young lover and an old husband, then, after a sigh or two, she said: "Since your cunning, the folly of my husband, my mother's lack of scruple and the wickedness of my confessor have combined to make me do what I would never have done on my own, I can only believe that some divine influence has willed this, and, as it is not for me to resist what heaven decrees, I surrender. And so I take you for my lord, and master, and guide. You must be everything to me—father, defender, and the sole source of all my happiness: and what my husband wanted for a night, I want him to have forever. Seek his friendship, then: go to church this morning, then come home to dine with us; you shall come and go as you will, and we shall be able to be together at any time without suspicion." When I heard this I was overwhelmed with tenderness, and hardly able to express anything of what I felt. But the result is that I am the happiest and most contented man in the world, and if neither death nor time destroy my happiness—the saints themselves shall call me blessed!

So much for Messer Nicia: he is a classic cuckold, subject to our scorn, our laughter. If it be argued in his defense that his original motive, a desire for an heir, is a valid one, it must be admitted that his means to achieve that end are neither proper nor virtuous. And while we are laughing we ought not to forget that the virtuous Lucrezia is no longer a human being by the end of the play. She has become a thing, an object to be manipulated by the various forces. Even her extreme virtue, her sense of obedience to her husband, her mother, her confessor, has been used for a vicious purpose. And she does not mind, for, as she has said to Callimaco, ". . . you shall come and go as you will, and we shall be able to be together at any time without suspicion." Machiavelli has made it quite clear that he does not want his audience to wax sentimental over Lucrezia while it is laughing at Messer Nicia. The horns of the cuckold cast a ludicrous shadow, and the shadow manages to taint all the rest of the characters of Machiavelli's play.

Other treatments of the cuckoldry theme exist in dramatic

comedy, but *They Knew What They Wanted* and *Mandragola* indicate clearly enough the extremes of treatment. Because a benevolent haze of sentimentality envelops the former play, the cuckold, the woman, even the cuckolder, solicit our sympathy at the end of the play. And the solicitation is successful. Tony is noble and understanding; Amy is noble, penitent, and regretful; even Joe is noble in his willingness to expiate his sin in any way. As the curtain falls, but before the house lights go on, there is much fumbling for handkerchiefs, much surreptitious dabbing at tear-filled eyes, much loud, manly blowing of masculine noses. The cold intellectuality of the latter play prohibits sentimentality and demands laughter, not tears. We laugh at Messer Nicia, the cuckold, because he has not only consented but also helped plan what has happened. If what he planned for one night is to go on for a thousand and one nights, our laughter is the more boisterous on that account. We laugh with Callimaco, the cuckolder, at the successful conclusion of his cleverly outrageous strategy. So far as Lucrezia is concerned, we think of her—if we think of her at all—as merely a rather attractive prize in this salacious game of sex-love. If Callimaco thinks the game is worth the effort he expends, why should we object? For our concern is not with the prize, but with the technique of winning; not with sex, but with strategy; not with romance and sentiment, but with chicanery and cleverness.

If *They Knew What They Wanted* and *Mandragola* indicate extreme treatments of the cuckoldry theme, the various versions of the Amphitryon story indicate the middle road of treatment. In all the versions, the cuckolder is Jupiter, the king of the gods, and all sorts of divine aids are his for the thinking. He can change his form at will; he can extend the night so that one night of love leaves nothing to be desired, even by a god; he can summon the brilliantly nimble-minded Mercury as an assistant; he can freely indulge his "nostalgia for mortality";

he can even contravene the biological law which maintains that a period of 280 days is normally necessary between conception and parturition. What chance has an ordinary mortal, even a great general of Thebes, against so formidable an antagonist?

Of the many versions of the play only four need concern us here: the Plautine, the Molière, the Dryden, and the S. N. Behrman adaptation of the Jean Giraudoux version. In the Plautus play, despite the many farcical elements, Amphitruo is regarded finally as a man who has been honored by a heavenly visitation. "Well," says he, after his maid Bromia has told him the startling events which followed the birth of twin sons to his wife, "well, I'm scarcely going to complain about being permitted to share my blessings with Jupiter." (An interesting comparison may be drawn between Amphitruo's problem and the problem of Saint Joseph in the Gospel according to Saint Matthew. Note particularly that Saint Joseph "was minded to put her away privily.") Amphitruo then orders the maid to prepare sacrificial vessels so that he can make offerings to the god. He also plans to consult with Tiresias, the soothsayer, about the affair, but Jupiter appears to him, tells him the whole story, advises him to have nothing to do with soothsayers, and then departs for heaven. A literal translation of Amphitruo's line after Jupiter's departure might be, "I shall do as you order." A freer translation which manages to convey far more closely the reverent tone of the original might well be, "Thy will be done." Dramatic audiences should not find it strange that reverence follows so closely on the heels of farce. The religious origins of drama and the theory of the sugar-coated pill of instruction would insure that such a combination would occasionally happen. It happened in Greek drama; it happened in Roman drama; *The Second Shepherd's Play* and *The Comedy of Errors* show that it can happen in English drama also.

The Molière and Dryden versions of the Amphitryon story have much in common with each other both dramatically and thematically. Dramatically, they have much in common with the Roman play; thematically, they never approach Plautus. As has been pointed out, Plautus enables us to gain insight into Amphitruo's state of mind after the divine revelation has been made. In both Molière and Dryden, Amphitryon remains mute after the revelation. Both seventeenth-century playwrights have their Sosias interrupt Jupiter's explanation with a comment about the god's cleverness. And the explanation is clever, to be sure, in both Dryden and Molière, even though the cleverness seems to detract from the divinity. Since both seventeenth-century versions are similar in content, only one need be cited. Dryden's Jupiter speaks from a machine after a second peal of thunder:

> Look up, Amphitryon, and behold, above,
> The impostor god, the rival of thy love;
> In thy own shape see Jupiter appear,
> And let that sight secure thy jealous fear.
> Disgrace, and infamy, are turned to boast;
> No fame, in Jove's concurrence, can be lost;
> What he enjoys, he sanctifies from vice,
> And by partaking, stamps into a price.
> 'Tis I who ought to murmur at my fate,
> Forced by my love my godhead to translate;
> When on no other terms I could possess,
> But by thy form, thy features, and thy dress.
> To thee were given the blessings that I sought,
> Which else, not all the bribes of heaven had bought.
> Then take into thy arms thy envied love,
> And, in his own despite, triumph o'er Jove.

At this point, Mercury says in an aside, "Amphitryon and Alcmena both stand mute, and know not how to take it." And well they might. It is bad enough for a couple to be deceived and cuckolded by a god who remains, as Plautus' Jupiter does, direct, blunt, and divine; it is most confusing to be deceived and cuckolded by a god who indulges in rhetorical play as he maintains that he, not Amphitryon, ought to be jealous. Sosia follows Mercury's aside with an aside of his own that is pertinent in this connection: "Our sovereign lord Jupiter is a sly companion; he knows how to gild a bitter pill." But Jupiter is interrupted only for a moment. He goes on to foretell the future:

> From this auspicious night shall rise an heir,
> Great like his sire, and like his mother fair:
> Wrongs to redress, and tyrants to disseize;
> Born for a world that wants a Hercules.
> Monsters, and monster-men he shall engage,
> And toil, and struggle, through an impious age.
> Peace to his labours shall at length succeed;
> And murmuring men, unwilling to be freed,
> Shall be compelled to happiness, by need.

Jupiter is carried back to heaven, and finally scabrous Sosia is left to sum up the salacious play. The speech cited below has not, of course, any counterpart in Plautus. Neither has it a counterpart in Molière. Only Dryden, it would seem, had a mind which could encompass such sophisticated smut. Sosia speaks:

> For let the wicked world say what they please,
> The fair wife makes her husband live at ease:
> The lover keeps him too; and but receives,
> Like Jove, the remnants that Amphitryon leaves.
> 'Tis true, the lady has enough in store,
> To satisfy those two, and eke two more:
> In fine, the man, who weighs the matter fully,
> Would rather be the cuckold than the cully.

Only to Dryden's Sosia is every man a pimp and every woman a whore; only to Dryden's Sosia are financial matters more important than morality; only Dryden's Sosia has a mind of such curious turn that he can maintain that the cuckold is better off than the cuckolder.

Molière, while not so salacious as Dryden, is naturally not so reverent as Plautus. Nor is there any reason he should have been. By the time of Plautus, Roman religion had started to lose its primal faith, and Plautus was not so devout as Ennius, for example. At the same time, he would not be nearly so skeptical as a Molière. Molière, in other words, treated the pagan divinities with pardonable freedom and easily avoided Dryden's failures of taste. I have cited the concluding speech from Dryden's play. Here, now, is the concluding speech from Molière's. Jupiter has vanished into the clouds, and Naucrates, a Theban captain, says, "Certainly I am enraptured at these brilliant remarks. . . ." At this point, Sosia interrupts:

> Gentlemen, will you please to follow my opinion? Embark not in these pretty congratulations: it is a bad investment; and pretty phrases are embarrassing on either side, in such a compliment. The great god Jupiter has done us much honour, and, no doubt, his goodness towards us is unequalled; he promises the certain felicity of a glorious fate, bearing a thousand blessings, and, that in our house shall be born a very mighty son. Nothing could be better than all this. But, in short, a truce to speeches, and let every one retire in peace. It is always best in these matters to say nothing.

Dryden has, I admit, a similar speech, but he gives it to Mercury, not Sosia (and that is psychologically important) and he does not use it to end his play. Molière's Sosia gives the best possible advice when he insists that in these matters it is always best to say nothing. If the conclusions of the three plays show differences which may be ascribed to differences in time of composition and place of national origin, the beginnings of the three plays show similar differences. The plot, or Jupiter, demands that night be lengthened. Plautus merely has Mercury direct a few words in an aside to the goddess of night. Molière developed an entire scene from an interview between Night and Mercury. The scene is witty, clever, and completely satisfying. Night has some scruples, but Mercury's glib tongue soon sweeps them away. While Molière is facetious at the expense of the gods, Dryden is merely lewd. Night and Mercury in Molière are two sophisticates engaging in delightful banter; in Dryden we get a conversation between a pander and a bawd. While time and place account for most of the differences among the three plays, we should not forget that taste, or Dryden's lack of it, accounts for many of the differences.

There is no failure of taste in the S. N. Behrman adaptation of the Jean Giraudoux *Amphitryon* 38. It had the undoubted advantage of having Alfred Lunt play the rule of Jupiter, Lynn Fontanne the role of Alkmena, and the redoubtable Sidney Greenstreet playing the minor, but delightful, role of a Trumpeter. This version has the Plautine myth (properly modified for a modern audience) without the heavy-handed treatment and with its own peculiar sense of reverence; it possesses Molière's sense of high comedy, but it never degenerates, as its predecessor unfortunately does on occasion, into farce; and it has all of Dryden's sophistication, but none of his scurrility. And it differs from the other versions in particular as well as general terms. While all four plays have a god as a cuckolder, Jupiter's presence has strikingly different results in the different versions. Jupiter's presence in Plautus leads inevitably and reverently to the birth of a divine hero; his presence in Molière succeeds in raising bedroom farce to the level of high comedy and leads to the birth of a semi-divine hero; his presence in Dryden creates, along with a potential sweeper of the Augean stables, a farcical triangle of an arrogant cuckolder, a shrewish strumpet, and a pompous cuckold. In *Amphitryon* 38, written, adapted, and produced in the sophisticated twentieth century, his presence leads, amazingly enough, to the exaltation of connubial love. Jupiter, disguised as Amphitryon, has spent the night with Alkmena and he is talking to Mercury about her constancy: "Nevertheless, I have discovered that human beings are not what the gods think them. Alkmena, the gentle—the tender Alkmena has the character of a rock. She is the true Prometheus!" The cynical Mercury interjects: "It isn't that she has character, she lacks imagination." A troubled Jupiter who seemingly never before had been aware of female fidelity answers musingly: "Yes, she lacks imagination and it's even possible that she isn't very intelligent. She is ambitious neither to shock nor to dazzle. But it's exactly this single-minded quality in her, this quality of constancy and devotion, against which our power is futile." Jupiter should have known. In a previous scene he had attempted, although disguised as Amphitryon, to come to her as a lover:

ALKMENA: I have a husband and he is evidently not here. And I receive no one in my bedroom who is not my husband. And not even him will I admit if he does not acknowledge his name. You're not very good at passionate disguises—it's not your metier.

JUPITER: Oh, at this hour, when everything between here and heaven is in disguise, may not your husband also disguise himself as a lover?

ALKMENA: Your insight, my friend, is not very keen if you think the night is only the day-time masked, the moon no more than a sun disguised, and that the love of a wife for her husband can be confused with an amour.

JUPITER: Wifely love is a duty. Duty is compulsion. And compulsion kills desire.

ALKMENA: Desire! Desire is a half god. We, here, worship only the major ones. The lesser gods we leave to the adolescent girls, to the casually married, to the fugitive romantics, the half-wives.

JUPITER: It is blasphemy to speak so even of a lesser god!

ALKMENA: In my secret heart I am more blasphemous even than that for I worship a god that doesn't exist at all. Shall I tell you who it is? It's the god of conjugal love, one that it never occurred to the gods to invent—they are so casual. If you come in behalf of Desire you ask me to betray a greater god for a lesser. If then you are a lover I am sorry but I must ask you to go on. . . . You are handsome and you have a good figure. Your voice is winning. Did it sound in behalf of fidelity I might love this voice. I might wish to be enclosed in those arms. Your mouth, too, I should say is dewy and ardent. But I shan't allow it to persuade me. I shall not open my door to a lover. Who are you?

JUPITER: Why can't your husband be your lover?

ALKMENA: Because a lover is closer always to love than he is to the object of his love. Because it is ill-bred to deceive your husband —even with himself. Because I like my windows open and my linen fresh.

At this point, Alkmena leaves him and goes inside. He stews and frets for a while as he discusses this contretemps with Mercury, and then he capitulates, admits that he is Amphitryon, goes through a ceremony which she commands, is informed that the gate was open all the time, and then, as "husband" not "lover," he is admitted. Yes, Jupiter should have known, but how could Jupiter the philanderer realize the importance of conjugal love to some women? After all, he had never faced the problem before. Perhaps that is what he has in mind when he says resignedly to Mercury. "For the first time, Mercury, I have a suspicion that a thoroughly first-rate god might make a thoroughly second-rate man."

First-rate god or second-rate man, Jupiter had succeeded in spending the night with Alkmena. Mercury, with his love of ceremony and with his detailed knowledge of his father's state of mind, had decided that Jupiter was entitled to another night of love. He had, therefore, announced formally to the winds and the waters that Alkmena would receive a visit from Jupiter. The first visit had been, of course, unannounced. It is Mercury's job to inform Alkmena of the visitation and prepare her to accept the honor. His job is far more difficult than he had imagined. He cannot convince her of the great honor that will be hers. He is getting nowhere when Alkmena's maid announces that Leda is coming for a visit. Leda's visit gives Mercury a chance to relax and Alkmena a chance to conceive a plan. Leda, having once experienced Jupiter, wants very much to experience him again. The two women have decided that Jupiter will appear to Alkmena in the guise of Amphitryon; as Leda puts it, "Your swan will be Amphitryon." Alkmena, without much difficulty, persuades Leda to take her place. Leda does, Amphitryon—the real one—returns home after leaving his troops just for a short time, Alkmena is convinced that he is Jupiter in disguise and sends him to her darkened bedroom where Leda is waiting. Now both husband and wife are quits. Both have unwittingly committed adultery. The only problem that remains is the actual appearance of Jupiter. By the time he appears, Alkmena is aware of the terrible error she has made in the Leda incident, and she fears that Jupiter will tell Amphitryon the truth. She asks Jupiter for permission to be alone with him, and the permission is readily granted. She wins him over in argument. He agrees not to impose his presence on her, and his agreement makes her suspicious that he has already been her lover, "because my knowledge of men leads me to believe that when they're as noble as this, it's because they're already satisfied." And so, in addition to granting her desire that he not impose upon her, he also grants her forgetfulness of all the things that she wants to forget. Mercury and Amphitryon return, Amphitryon and Alkmena are informed that Alkmena will bear a son, and are asked to name him Hercules, "to please me." Jupiter then says, "and I shall be his . . . godfather . . ." and joins with Mercury in saying, ". . . and so will destiny be fulfilled!"

And destiny has certainly taken a devious road toward fulfilment. The cuckolder will become a "godfather"; the unwitting cuckold has become an unwitting adulterer; and the third member of this triangle, the virtuous wife who worships the god of conjugal love, has been granted forgetfulness of all that she wants to forget, except for one kiss which Jupiter carefully places this side of oblivion. We don't mind that Jupiter has that one minor victory, for this is a strange play; the object of our laughter is not the cuckold, but the cuckolder. And this strange twist on a traditional theme has been accomplished by the articulateness and strength of character of a virtuous woman. Connubial love, with a slight assist from forgetfulness, has triumphed over divine lechery, and Amphitryon and Alkmena remain, in Jupiter's words, "a small island of fidelity."

A small island of fidelity can exist at the end of a comedy; it can even exist at the beginning of a comedy. It is, unfortunately perhaps, almost impossible to write comedies or tragedies about unthreatened happy marriages. A threat to the marriage or to the prospect of marriage must exist before tension can be achieved, before conflict can be established. The comedy most frequently is the result of the successful overcoming of the threat. Comic opera and Hollywood do not own the copyright on the ancient comic theme of boy-meets-girl, boy-loses-girl, boy-gets-girl. Romantic comedy of this sort can be traced in English literature at least as far back as John Lyly and William Shakespeare. Even when Shakespeare wrote a comedy in what he considered the classic vein, like *The Comedy of Errors*, he ended it in the romantic tradition by restoring two marriages which time and chance had caused to founder, and by promising the early celebration of still a third. In *The Way of the World*, where the primary focus is on wit not drama, the prospect of a marriage is the delightful and romantic conclusion. Surely the proposal and acceptance scene between Millamant and Mirabell comes as close to romantic drama as is possible in this brilliantly cold comedy of manners. Indeed, I might even go so far as to maintain that after all of the conditions and articles and provisos have been agreed to by this admirable pair, and after Mirabell has said, "Then we're agreed. Shall I kiss your Hand upon the Contract?" we have witnessed a scene of passion between two brilliant and witty people. I, for one, would be willing to sacrifice emotion-racked adolescent lovemaking for the classical restraint involved in Millamant's "Well—I think—I'll endure you. . . . Well, you ridiculous thing you, I'll have you—I won't be kiss'd, nor I won't be thank'd— Here kiss my Hand tho'— So, hold your Tongue now, don't say a Word."

We do have plays, however, in which marriage seems the source of sorrow not happiness. When we first see Sir Peter Teazle in *The School for Scandal*, he is bemoaning his married state: "When an old bachelor marries a young wife, what is he to expect? 'Tis now six months since Lady Teazle made me the happiest of men—and I have been the most miserable dog ever since!" Indeed, Sir Peter seems to be in a horrible state, much worse off than we would expect even from the Greek poet's diatribe on the subject of marriage: "Marriage brings a man only two happy days: the day he beds his bride and the day he buries her." Sir Peter is probably too old ever to know the second happy day, and he did not have a chance to know the first: "We tift a little going to church, and came to a quarrel before the bells had done ringing. I was more than once nearly choked with gall during the honeymoon, and had lost all comfort before my friends had done wishing me joy." Much of Sir Peter's dialogue in the play is taken up with his marital difficulties. So deeply does he feel his problems that he frequently repeats himself, but in this comedy of manners repetition does not preclude wit: "Ah! Master Rowley, when an old bachelor marries a young wife, he deserves—no—the crime carries its punishment along with it." He may feel deeply but, as the hesitation in the above quotation indicates, he feels even more deeply about the necessity of expressing himself wittily and epigrammatically. And his predicament seems unbearable. Note his first conversation in the play with Lady Teazle:

SIR PETER T.: Lady Teazle, Lady Teazle, I'll not bear it!

LADY T.: Sir Peter, Sir Peter, you may bear it or not, as you please; but I ought to have my own way in everything, and what's more, I will, too. What! though I was educated in the country, I know very well that women of fashion in London are accountable to nobody after they are married.

SIR PETER T.: Very well, ma'am, very well;—so a husband is to have no influence, no authority?

LADY T.: Authority! No, to be sure:—if you wanted authority over me, you should have adopted me, and not married me: I am sure you were old enough.

Not even the bitter cruelty of her attack on the difference in their ages seems to bother him overmuch. You might even say that he enjoys their daily jangles, for he says, after her departure: "So—I have gained much by my intended expostulation: yet, with what a charming air she contradicts everything I say, and how pleasingly she shows her contempt for my authority! Well, though I can't make her love me, there is great satisfaction in quarreling with her; and I think she never appears to such an advantage as when she is doing everything in her power to plague me." Yet the end of the play shows that Lady Teazle has learned her lesson, and that Sir Peter has learned his. They seem destined for a happy marriage after the curtain falls, no matter how stormy had been the on-stage dramatics. And to crown the comedy there will be another marriage, for Charles Surface and Maria are to be married on the morrow.

For when love enters comedy—at least since the time of Shakespeare—it must result in marriage. Even Oscar Wilde, who defied conventions of manners, morals, and dramaturgy, was not brave enough to flout this one, even though he may have intended to satirize it. *The Importance of Being Earnest* ends with prospective marriages between Algernon and Cecily, between Jack and Gwendolen. These potential nuptials cause us little surprise, for we have been expecting such an ending ever since the young people found one another. The third potential marriage is thrown in either for lagniappe or satire or possibly both. We know about it through four words of dialogue and six of stage direction. Canon Chasuble, who normally speaks metaphorically, speaks most directly: "(*to Miss Prism*) Laetitia! (*Embraces her.*)" Miss Prism needs three words, but her meaning is clear: "(*enthusiastically*). Frederick! At Last!" Even if Wilde did intend the third marriage as a touch of satire on the convention, it seems at least as logical as the spate of marriages which concludes *Twelfth Night* and *As You Like It*, and no more satirical than the marriages which conclude *Measure For Measure*.

Nor is the convention confined to plays of the sixteenth, seventeenth, eighteenth, and nineteenth centuries. The twentieth century retains it (occasionally in modified form to be sure) because it is dramaturgically convenient and financially lucrative to do so. W. Somerset Maugham ends *The Circle* with the elopement of Elizabeth and Teddie. The fact that Elizabeth is already married to someone else doesn't seem to bother anyone. After all, if Arnold will permit Elizabeth a divorce, she and Teddie will probably marry. If Arnold is unwilling, Elizabeth and Teddie will probably enjoy a permanent, if illegal, liaison. It has all happened before. Lady Kitty, Arnold's mother, had deserted Arnold's father in similar circumstances. Her life since her elopement could not be accurately described as calmly contented, yet she encourages her daughter-in-law to run away with another man. Her reason may be summed up in one of her epigrammatic utterances: "The tragedy of love isn't death or separation. One gets over them. The tragedy of love is indifference." Arnold may be indifferent to Elizabeth or, rather, aware of her only as her actions may affect his career; Teddie is aware of her as a person, as an individual, as an object of love. When Elizabeth asks him what he would do if he were in the same situation as Arnold, his answer is far from indifferent: "You have very pretty blue eyes, Elizabeth. I'd black first one and then the other. And after that we'd see." Teddie may be a brute, a caveman, not quite a gentleman, but no one could accuse him of indifference.

Philip Barry's *Holiday* also ends with the prospect of marriage. The marriage is not the one we had expected from the beginning of the play, but it is kept in the same family. Perhaps indifference is the reason that the marriage does not take place as originally planned. Julia is not indifferent to what Johnny can do, she is not indifferent to convention or to what other people think, but she is indifferent to Johnny himself, his hopes, his dreams, his unconventional ideas. Her sister, Linda, is indifferent to almost all the other things, but she is not indifferent to Johnny. She would not be so low, so devious, so flouting of convention as to attempt to steal away her sister's fiancé, but once the engagement is broken, once she is convinced that Julia is not sad at the development but actually relieved, she sets out to pursue Johnny, to catch him, to marry him. We feel sure she will be successful. Her single-minded devotion deserves no less.

Sally Middleton in John Van Druten's *The Voice of the Turtle* may be, as Louis Kronenberger has suggested, the first of the non-virginal ingénues to decorate the stage. For despite her two previous affairs, despite the one she has during the play, despite the surface sophistication, she is still emotionally adolescent, still sweet, simple, and girlish. The entire function of the play is, I believe, to show the maturation process. By the end of the third act, she has managed to get over the first big hurdle. She no longer stops Bill Page from saying, "I love you," because she wants to keep the affair "gay"; she is even able to say that she loves him. We are sure that she and Bill will marry; we are also sure that the marriage will be between two mature human beings: Sally will not be a child bride. Bill, who is able to put up with much, could not put up with that.

To find musical comedies in the twentieth century ending in marriages is not surprising. A modern musical comedy is so often a heady blend of Ruritanian romance and Ziegfield Follies that the entire show frequently seems like a flamboyant wedding rehearsal. But there should be some exceptions, and surely one of the exceptions should be a musical comedy "Based on a story and characters by Damon Runyon." Jo Swerling, Abe Burrows, and Frank Loesser put this show together and called it *Guys and Dolls*. The two leading male characters are Sky Masterson, a big-time gambler who is called Sky because that's how high he bets, and Nathan Detroit, the operator of the oldest established permanent floating crap game in New York. The two leading female characters are Miss Adelaide, the star of the revue at the Hot Box Club, and Miss Sarah Brown of the Save-A-Soul Mission. The odds against any of these characters getting married seem very high. They seem higher when you realize that Adelaide, "the well-known fiancée," has been engaged to Nathan Detroit for fourteen years. They seem astronomical when we hear a piece of the dialogue between Adelaide and Sky:

ADELAIDE: What about you men? Why can't you marry people like other people do and live normal like people? Have a home, with—wallpaper and book ends.

SKY: (*sadly*) No, Miss Adelaide.

ADELAIDE: What do you mean—No?

SKY: Guys like Nathan Detroit and—yeah, Sky Masterson— we don't belong in a life like that. So when dolls get mixed up with guys like us, it's no good.*

Even with the odds as high as they are, two marriages take place. Sky Masterson marries Miss Sarah Brown and switches from gambling to singing hymns and playing the bass drum in the mission band. Nathan Detroit is going to marry Miss Adelaide, and has already made the switch. He no longer operates a crap game; he now runs a news stand. Here, as so often in comedy, marriage and respectability go hand in hand. Respectability to Miss Adelaide means, among other things, that she no longer has to suffer from her psychosomatic cold; respectability to Nathan merely means that his psychosomatic cold is just starting.

The relationship between the sexes provides other sources of comedy and laughter. The hen-pecked or hag-ridden husband has frequently been the object of mirth and at least once, and this in Noel Coward's *Blithe Spirit,* he overcomes his adversaries to the delight of all masculine members of the audience. But the household that contains a hen-pecked husband has always seemed to me, perhaps incorrectly, to be devoid of love, devoid of sex. I am sure that comedy can ensue from such a situation; I am equally sure that such comedy has nothing to do with love or sex.

The horns of the cuckold may cast a ludicrous shadow, but so do the horns of the lecherous old goat. The old goat with a yen for pretty young things is always treated as a comic figure, but his female counterpart, the old woman who still feels the stirring of elemental impulses, is treated rather differently. There are exceptions like Lady Wishfort in *The Way of the World* and the character that Margaret Dumont portrayed so long and so well in Marx Brothers motion pictures, but most lecherous old women are treated as pathetic, not comic, figures. Here the double standard obtains: There are no masculine Lorelei Lees in the dramatist's comic repertoire; even Schnitzler's Anatol fails to qualify.

And the reason that love and sex are so often sources of the comic is easy to explain. Love is a serious thing which makes the world go round. It can be a source of tragedy, of melodrama, of pathos. It causes adolescents to moon, mature people to stare forgetfully and unseeingly into space, older people to wax sentimental. Because it is so serious, so important, it is able easily to bear our laughter. All important things can. Only the picayune and the proud cannot endure laughter; and love, true love, is never picayune or proud. Love is better for having endured laughter, and we are more perceptive for having laughed. I do not mean that love has been completely purged of its excesses or that we have been completely purged of ours. If the truth were known, both love and we are secretly happy with our excesses, but laughter makes us understand that they are excesses. Mooning, staring forgetfully, waxing sentimental must be controlled and laughter is an excellent controlling factor. That is why love and laughter go hand in hand. They need each other; they deserve each other; and we need them both.

And perhaps there is one reason why a comic writer should of all others be the least excused for deviating from nature, since it may not be always so easy for a serious poet to meet with the great and the admirable; but life everywhere furnishes an accurate observer with the ridiculous.
—HENRY FIELDING in the Author's Preface to *Joseph Andrews*

We the people are not amused

The forces and pressures that attempt to keep the comic spirit down are felt in the land; the voices that attempt to still the comic spirit are heard in the land. More important, perhaps, they have always been felt, they have always been heard. So strong are the forces and pressures, so loud and repetitious are the voices, that we unconsciously use the voices' clichés when we try to deal with matters of moment. "This is no laughing matter," says the parent as he attempts to remonstrate with his child. Most often, however, it is a laughing matter. "Wipe that smile off your face," says the hardboiled top sergeant to the recruit who has yet to become accustomed to military discipline. With civilian freedom still firm in the memory, few recruits can prevent the smile from rising to the lips; only fear of that vast unknown which is mysteriously called military discipline prevents the belly laugh.

"Now let's be serious for a moment." For a moment? When aren't we serious? Has any aspect of our lives not been perverted by the infection of seriousness? The answer seems to be, "No." Politics? Peter Finley Dunne and Will Rogers are dead, but the memory of the 1952 presidential election in which seriousness crushed wit is still very much alive. Religion? Bishop Sheen had the rare ability to make theology amusing, and his Hooper rating declined. Sex? The Kinsey Reports and psychoanalytical sententiousness have supplanted *Is Sex Necessary?* and Mae West. Literature? To the contemporary literary critic, irony is no laughing matter. Science and technology? We must catch up with the Russians; we have no time for Gulliver's visit to the Academy at Lagado; we have, it seems, no time for comedy. (We seem, however, to have plenty of time for gadgets.) Business and commerce? "I think we ought to promote Jones; Smith doesn't seem to take matters seriously enough," and making money is a serious business. Social problems? "If we're not careful, we may offend some minority group." And so it goes.

But let's stop there before we begin to take these jeremiads seriously ourselves. Comedy's obituary has been written before —many times. Comedy's interment service has been read before—many times. But the ancient art has survived before and will again. For along with the voices that attempt to keep comedy down, another voice is heard in the land. It is not heard, to be sure, by those of faint heart or little faith; it is not heard by those who are not attuned to the future; it is heard only by those who know that nothing genuine has to fear laughter. And what do we call this voice? The answer cannot be given in a word, for this voice has many different inflections.

One inflection is called Mort Sahl, and attempts, successfully I believe, to prove that politicians and politics are fit subjects for comedy. Sahl is not alone, to be sure, any more than Will Rogers was alone, but surely we may cite him as one of the leaders of the post-McCarthy school of political satirists. Some of the other leaders of this movement deserve mention, too. They are not necessarily comedians, but they do produce, on occasion, comedy, and we can ask little more than that. James Reston of the *New York Times* sometimes views politics with satire as well as with alarm. Bill Mauldin, formerly of the *St. Louis Post-Dispatch* and now of the *Chicago Sun-Times*, has demonstrated that his cartoons can be as perceptive and comic in cold war as in hot, that he can deal with world problems as well as platoon politics. Walt Kelly, Al Capp, and Jules Feiffer occasionally deal with politics and are occasionally clever enough to make us believe temporarily that politics and politicians are indigenous to the comic page, not the editorial page, of our newspaper.

All of these men, Feiffer, Capp, Kelly, Mauldin, Reston, and Sahl, have the kind of satiric bite that all true political and social comedy should possess. The extreme danger of political and social satire is that the satirist in making his attack on one object may by contrast tend to sentimentalize or ennoble that object's opposite. It is difficult to be satiric at the expense of the Republican party without implying that the Democratic party is on the side of the angels; it is difficult to satirize the organization known as Americans for Democratic Action without the implication that all is sweetness and light in the John Birch Society. Most good political and social satirists are aware of the dangerous pitfalls. By careful examination of all the facets of the particular political or social issue under discussion, they manage to avoid sentimentality—most of the time; they manage to praise virtue and condemn vice—most of the time. And what is most important, they manage to do all these things without avoiding a decision on the issue of the moment. They do not sacrifice principle; they do take a definite stand.

I have naturally omitted many political and social satirists as representative of the type as those I have mentioned. One, however, I cannot omit. His name is Dick Gregory. He has all the equipment that any great stand-up comedian should have. He has presence, a style of his own, a most perceptive eye, and a devastating wit. He can handle politics and he can handle social problems, and he does both brilliantly. But his major target is the evil that can and does reside in the human heart, and in this field he produces comedy that is almost too great for laughter. He is young, and he is new, and his promise is greater perhaps than his present accomplishment. With the knowledge of many seemingly great young comedians who started out brilliantly but rapidly faded from the public scene, I find it hard to get too enthusiastic over a brilliant start. I feel sure, however, that Dick Gregory's talent is not going to wither on the vine.

That politics can be once more a subject of comedy is heartening in the extreme. Even more heartening is the philosophy which permits such a situation. At the risk of oversimplification one thing may be said. When comedians no longer deal satirically with politics, they are restrained by two fears. One is ignoble, perhaps, but human; the other is altruistic, but cowardly. The first fear obtains in a political dictatorship; here the comedian feels that he is wiser to avoid political satire and survive than to use political satire and be silenced. The second fear obtains when the comedian sees objects of satire in his government but refrains from pointing them out lest a worse government be visited upon his country and his people. Fortunately, despite the tensions which are gripping the world, the comedians in this country and in the rest of the Western democracies seemingly have rid themselves of these fears. These nations are the stronger for it, because in politics and government—as well as in most other areas of human life—high comedy is to be preferred to low seriousness.

Another inflection of this voice is called Shelley Berman or Bob Newhart or Joey Bishop or any of the other comedians, writers, and cartoonists who portray themselves as Everyman overwhelmed by a gadget civilization. Berman and Newhart and Bishop rarely smile themselves, but their dilemmas cause laughter in their audiences, who have so often experienced the same dilemmas themselves. In their category, but with a difference, belong Alan King and Sam Levenson. The irascible King is beaten by the gadget civilization and suburbia, but he refuses to admit defeat. He snarls, he screams, he is apoplectic in his rage, but he, too, is overwhelmed. He may go down fighting, but down he goes. The quality of redemption which comedy needs is supplied by the realization that he will rise and fight and be overwhelmed once more.

The benign and benevolent Sam Levenson smiles, giggles, and laughs aloud at the dilemmas produced by the attempt to raise and educate children in this day and age. His background as a teacher undoubtedly has instilled in him the realization that if you do not laugh loudly you will go mad quietly. His pointed commentary on the difference between his own childhood and that of his children gives him a double-edged weapon. The younger members feel sure he is exaggerating the poverty of his childhood, so they laugh. The older members feel sure that he is exaggerating the affluence—and the influence—of the child of today, so they laugh. As he reaps the reward of his double approach, he perhaps must wonder, as Berman, Newhart, Bishop, and King must also wonder, if in this civilization's enhancement of the materialistic it hasn't succeeded in degrading the spiritual forces which comedy and life both desperately need.

For these five men, and other comedians like them, represent perhaps the classical notion that comedy should hold the mirror up to nature. They deal with foibles and follies, their own as well as those of others. They do not provide explicit remedies—although Bishop may be an exception in this—but they do imply remedies, or rather one remedy. Their one remedy seems to be that man must control the gadgets, and the gadgets should never control man. They may appear, at first blush, to be reactionaries seeking a return to a less complex, less mechanical age. This appearance is momentary and, perhaps, illusionary. Berman wants airplanes, Newhart wants automobiles, Bishop wants Las Vegas, King wants baby sitters, Levenson wants audio-visual aids, but they are wise enough to realize that these mechanical and materialistic symbols are merely aids to the full life, not the full life itself. Their comedy seems to imply that materialistic conveniences taken in moderation are good things, but when all life is dedicated to their pursuit, then the pursuer becomes the captured. The sable-lined cage may be comfortable and convenient, but something had to be sacrificed to obtain it. That something, they seem to say, is freedom—and here they find common cause with the political comedians—and when you lose freedom to act, you lose other important freedoms like the freedom to laugh.

Perhaps I probe too deeply into the motivations of these men. Perhaps I am seeing what I elsewhere disparagingly termed the Pagliacci syndrome. I do not think so. These men are not perhaps great thinkers, but they are exceedingly sensitive men. Their extreme sensitivity has caused them to choose as subjects of comedy and objects of satire the conveniences that we feel we must have, which soon turn into the jailers which we do not want. So these men are, in a sense, most successful. By attacking the materialistic conveniences which they enjoy, they make the best of both possible worlds. They control the conveniences; the conveniences do not control them. They wear their gadgets with a difference.

And fortunately these men are young. I say "fortunately" not because I believe that there is any particular virtue in being young, but because we have heard so much in recent years about the aging comedians in our society. We have been sadly told—and these tears are not glycerine, they're genuine—that there is no longer a source of supply for new comedians. We are told that vaudeville is dead, burlesque is dead. There is no place where the young comedian can get the necessary training, the necessary time, the necessary knowledge of an audience, so that he can polish his art. And if, by some lucky stroke of circumstance, a young comedian does get his act polished and fit for presentation, overexposure on television soon exhausts his entire repertoire. We are told that Red Buttons, Sid Caesar, George Gobel, and Jackie Gleason are all victims of the cavernous maw of television which devours material, particularly comic material, faster than it can be created. We may disregard the illogicality of the last clause as we point out that Berman, Newhart, Bishop, King, and Levenson, and many others like them, have given the lie to the prophets of gloom. Even the "victims" mentioned above appear from time to time on the stage, in the motion pictures, and even on television, looking and acting anything but victimized.

We have good young comedians, and we have good mature comedians, too. (I carefully avoid the use of the word "old"; I somehow feel that the term "old comedian" is a contradiction in terms. If this be sentimentality, make the most of it.) Jack Benny, Bob Hope, Jimmy Durante, Red Skelton (in many ways the most versatile of living comedians), continue to use their tried-and-true repertoires with great success, continue to improvise new routines, also with great success. As I have not attempted to list all of the young comedians, so have I omitted many of the still successful mature comedians.

And note well that I have listed only males. Even an anti-feminist would have to admit that an innovation of our time is the emergence of the stand-up female comedian, that another inflection of our voice has a contralto's or a soprano's range. In the past, female comedians were used in skits, in situation comedies, as foils for the men, or using the men as foils. In that last connection, Gracie Allen, Portland Hoffa, and Jane Ace ruled supreme. Now we see Phyllis Diller, Kay Ballard, Pat Carroll, and others like them, taking a place in what was formerly regarded as territory reserved for men only. The first reaction to this female invasion was analogous to Dr. Johnson's remark about the lady preacher; the second reaction was one of great pleasure, and great amusement; the last reaction was one of delighted acceptance. In comedy, as in so many other areas of life, the double standard is as extinct as the dodo. And it is fortunate that it is. We need these female stand-up comedians to give their views on the materialistic, mechanical civilization that threatens to engulf women even more than it threatens to engulf men. For when the money managers and the wizards of Madison Avenue began to realize that women control, in this country at least, the bulk of the purchasing power, they began to direct their siren song at the women, to create their gadgets for the beauty shop and the kitchen.

For along with politics and gadgetry as objects of satire, as sources of comedy, we may add that arcane area called economics or business or commerce. Perhaps the greatest statement on the subject of economics was that made by Jimmy Durante in the middle 1930's. His statement undoubtedly owed something to Joe Cook's routine about the Three Hawaiians, but it had a unique quality that only Durante's delivery could afford it. If memory serves, Durante growled into the microphone, "I'm supposed to talk about the depression.

What's a depression? A depression's a dent. And what's a dent? A dent's a hole. And what's a hole? A hole's nothin'. And if you think I'm gonna stand up here and talk about nothin', you're crazy."

We're more sophisticated than that now, but I doubt that we're any funnier. But once again we find economics and business and commerce funny. Even the financial pages of some of our newspapers, whose only pictorial alleviation from columns of statistics is an occasional graph, have started to publish a cartoon called "Blue Chips," by a cartoonist called Brickman. The editorial page of the *Wall Street Journal* contains a cartoon and some not-very-funny jokes. But at least they're trying. If interest in financial matters can be made comic, what avenue is closed?

The area of commerce which should be most susceptible to comic analysis is the advertising industry. And advertising has been carefully examined by both comic writers and comic performers. The performers, however, seem to operate under a handicap which is almost insurmountable, particularly when these performers work in radio and television. After all, the money that pays the performers' salaries is advertising money. Any reasonable man knows—or soon discovers—that you do not with impunity bite the hand that feeds you. So Henry Morgan was sidetracked, Bob and Ray were rendered antiseptic, and then came the crowning irony. The advertising men discovered that the public *liked* advertisements that didn't take themselves too seriously; the public *wanted* the bitter pill of advertising sugar—or spice—coated with comedy. Cartoons replaced the hard sell; carefully contrived mistakes appeared in television commercials; even Bob and Ray were put back to work. But the fear and the handicap remain. Few television or radio comedians poke fun at an advertiser's product unless the fun has been carefully inserted in the script by the practiced hand of an advertising copy writer. As a result, the comedy that now appears in advertising is just a bit disingenuous, not quite real. The bars that imprisoned the comic imagination in this field have been dispensed with, but a leash remains. The sponsors and the advertising moguls do not seem to realize—if, indeed, they care—that freedom does not admit of degree.

The comic writers, however, do not seem to work under such a restraint, particularly if they write for periodicals which brook no infringement upon their editorial policy. As a result, S. J. Perelman, one of the great comic writers of our time, if not the greatest, has a field day when he contemplates the excesses of perfume advertisements, department-store effusions, and soda-fountain menus. Perelman, of course, is not limited to the area of advertising; his range is tremendously wide: little of the comic in the human circumstance escapes him. Afflicted with total recall, possessed of a deadly accurate eye and a devastatingly accurate ear, he is our most brilliant satiric commentator on manners and morals. We owe him a debt for his comments in many areas, but because he stands almost alone as a satirist of advertising, we are particularly grateful for his perception, wit, and satire in this field.

So the voice has many inflections, some new, some restored, some which have been always with us. But there is one inflection of the comic voice that used to be heard everywhere but which the pressures have stilled almost to a whisper. It has not been silenced completely, nor will it be, for it has too much tradition behind it, too much strength in it, too much of a future before it. Already there is evidence that this inflection will be heard everywhere once more, but many restraints on its freedom still exist. What is this inflection, and what are some of its restraints? Perhaps the answers to these questions should be approached circuitously; perhaps we can start with an episode that may be interpreted as a parable is interpreted.

Some years ago I picked up a copy of Leo Rosten's *The*

Return of Hyman Kaplan in my favorite bookstore. The dust jacket made me, I recall, very happy. In an age of change, some things, and important things at that, had remained the same. Hyman Kaplan had returned, and the Great Name still flaunted its colors bravely: the letters in red, the letters' outlines in blue, the ever youthful, ever aspiring, stars still separated the letters and were still in green. In my first flush of enthusiasm I bought the book, I carried it home, I started to read it.

While I was reading it, I had the uneasy feeling that something was happening to me that had not happened for a long time. I found myself laughing, laughing out loud, to the complete amazement of my wife and children. Now they were not amazed that I was laughing while reading a book. After all, they know I do that frequently. In fact, their long-suffering sighs and long-suffering set faces have told me often that they wished I wouldn't. They were amazed this time because I wasn't stopping them as they went about their various tasks and pleasures to read them portions of the book that was making me laugh.

Other times when I laugh as I read, I insist that all work and play stop as I regale them with this comic episode or with that joke. I wasn't doing that now. The reason I didn't insist on reading to them from *The Return of Hyman Kaplan* was a very simple one. I am a very limited man. I can't wiggle my ears, pick up pencils with my toes, or imitate dialects. If you can't imitate dialects, there is little, if any, point in trying to read aloud from any story about Hyman Kaplan. As the old bromide has it, it certainly loses something in translation.

But all this merely explains why my family was amazed. It doesn't explain the uneasy feeling that I had while I was laughing. I think that I can explain that uneasy feeling, and I feel that it is relatively easy to do so. I was uneasy, I think, because I was laughing at a dialect story. Now there is absolutely no reason why I or anyone else shouldn't laugh at dialect humor—I think. Nor is there any reason why I or anyone else should feel uneasy about laughing at dialect humor—again I think. Or let me put it another way, and then I won't have to qualify my remarks with any *I think's:* thirty years ago we wouldn't have felt uneasy as we laughed at dialect humor. Indeed, we would have expected dialect comedians on any vaudeville bill we saw, on any radio program we listened to, in any humorous book we read.

Examples to prove the point are easy to find, and we don't have to limit ourselves to an artificial span of thirty years. We could go back to Shakespeare, we could go back to Chaucer, we could go back to the Bible and the problem (not always humorously resolved) of pronouncing *shibboleth* correctly, but Shakespeare seems a good place to start. Millions of people have seen Sir Lawrence Olivier's motion-picture production of Shakespeare's *Henry V*. Many more millions have seen stage productions of the same play. In it there are many comic scenes, most of them made comic by dialect humor. Shakespeare places in Henry's army—perhaps in an effort to point out that Henry had united Britain—four captains. One of the captains, the immortal Fluellen, is a Welshman. His dialect makes us laugh. The second captain is Macmorris, an Irishman. His dialect makes us laugh. The third captain is Jamy, a Scot. His dialect makes us laugh. The fourth captain's name is Gower. He is an Englishman. He has no dialect and he does not make us laugh. Indeed, he is the most forgettable character in the play.

Now I don't believe that any Welshman, Irishman, or Scot has been hurt by the dialect humor in the play; but a modern writer, writing for television or the motion pictures, would think twice before he put such characters, speaking such dialects, in his television or screen play. He would think twice, that is, and then decide to leave them out, particularly if the episode demanded that these characters be comic butts or comic villains. It is still barely permissible to have sympathetic comic characters speak in dialect, but not a comic butt or a comic villain. In fact, it would seem that the only comic butts and comic villains available these days are dialectless, white, Anglo-Saxon Protestants. And if they ever get properly organized (and they should just in order to be able to use the delightful acronymic title of WASPS) all the comic villains will disappear from the face of the earth. But to return to Shakespeare. He doesn't confine his use of dialect humor to *Henry V*. He uses it in *The Merry Wives of Windsor*, in *Henry IV, Part I*, and in *The Taming of The Shrew*, and these three do not exhaust all the possibilities in the Shakespeare canon. I don't think that the plays which contain dialect humor should be suppressed, or banned, or avoided on that account.

Nor is the use of dialect humor among the so-called classic authors confined to Shakespeare. Congreve and Sheridan use it in their plays. The country bumpkin in many eighteenth-century plays, speaking his quaint rustic dialect, is frequently a source of amusement. The ready ears of Dickens and Thackeray made the nineteenth-century novel a storehouse of dialect humor. Oscar Wilde raised the diction of upper-class Englishmen to such a high pitch that what started out as normal speech became dialect and comic. Both Shaw's *Pygmalion* and the Lerner and Lowe *My Fair Lady* would lose much if the dialect humor were removed.

But *Pygmalion* and *My Fair Lady* bring us back to the twentieth century, and the twentieth century produced *The Return of Hyman Kaplan*, a book that made me feel uneasy as I laughed. I have said that thirty years ago I wouldn't have felt uneasy. Let's go back and see why. Take a year in the 1930's, take 1934. What were we doing for laughs then? Remember that vaudeville, if not dead, was dying. Sound movies and the popularity of radio had seen to that. Well, what did we do for laughs? I know what millions of Americans did. At seven o'clock, five nights a week, owners of motion picture theaters cursed an unkind fate. The American Telephone and Telegraph Company noted a decline in the number of calls. Doorbells ceased ringing for fifteen minutes. Ma stopped yelling at Pa. Pa stopped yelling at the kids. Grandpa adjusted his ear trumpet. And all this happened—making allowance for local time zones—from Presque Isle, Maine, to San Diego, California. What was going on to cause this eerie stillness to blanket the country? It was perfectly simple. There was a radio program on at that time to which all America listened. Its name was *Amos 'n' Andy*, and it depended for its comic effect almost completely on dialect humor. The Fresh Air Taxi Cab, "I'se regusted," the Kingfish, Madam Queen, all became national bywords. Sure we laughed *at* Andy and *at* the Kingfish. Equally sure is the fact that we laughed *with* the long-suffering Amos. Sure they were stereotypes, and many thoughtful Negroes and many thoughtful whites wondered, some silently, some aloud, if there weren't something a trifle sadistic in our laughter. Perhaps there was—although I doubt it—but *Amos 'n' Andy* made the depression a little easier to bear, made the problems of the day a little easier to cope with. *Calvin and the Colonel* had, I feel sure, no such salutary effect.

Amos 'n' Andy was over at 7:15, and thirty minutes remained for the phone calls, for the doorbells, for the minor errands, for mother to do the dishes (of course you could do the dishes and listen to the radio at the same time, but not while *Amos 'n' Andy* was on), for Pa and the kids to get the aggression out of their systems, and for Grandpa to dig the wax out of his ears. Then, at 7:45, all action around the house froze again. Another radio program came on. Its name was *The Rise of the Goldbergs,* and it depended for its comic effect almost completely on dialect humor. The sound of the window being raised (one of the few sounds on the program not in dialect), "Yoohoo, Mrs. Bloom," the problems and pleasures of Sammy, Rosie, Jake and, above all, Mollie, became national bywords. Sure the characters were stereotyped, and many thoughtful Jews and many thoughtful gentiles wondered, some silently, some aloud, if there weren't something sadistic in our laughter. Perhaps there was—although I doubt it—but the Goldbergs remained firmly rooted in the hearts of the American radio audience, in the hearts of Americans. Somehow *Mrs. G. Goes to College* seems, to me at least, eminently forgettable.

Amos 'n' Andy and *The Goldbergs* were on the air five nights a week, and there was another phenomenon, no less precious, who appeared but once a week on Wednesday evenings at nine o'clock. His name was Fred Allen, and he was Irish, but he was also a Yankee with a nasal Yankee twang. He was popular, very popular, and so was his show. One of the funniest segments of his show was his weekly visit with the denizens of a place that he called "Allen's Alley." Every one depended upon dialect humor for comic effect. There was Ajax Cassidy of the Irish brogue; the irascible Titus Moody, who was as downeast as Aroostook County potatoes; the pompous and flatulent Senator Claghorn, who was a better parody of some Southern members of congress than even Al Capp's Senator Jack S. Phogbound; and Mrs. Nussbaum, played so brilliantly by Minerva Pious that many a man envied her never-appearing husband, Pierre. We laughed because of these people and not, I think, with condescension.

There were other dialect comedians on the radio—Lou Holtz, Jack Pearl, Eddie Anderson—but surely I have mentioned enough to prove the point that we used to laugh, and not uneasily, at dialect humor. Perhaps there was at times a touch of the sadistic, a touch of the condescending, in our laughter, but the laughter was, I think, far healthier than that which found hilarious the transvestitism of Jack Lemmon and Tony Curtis in *Some Like It Hot*, healthier than that which found hilarious the sophisticated attitude toward violence and sex that marked the sick joke.

Notice that I just went back to the thirties to prove my point. I could have gone back in American social history much further, for the dialect comedian has been the staple of American humor at least since the revolution. The Yankee Peddler, the backwoodsman, the supercilious Englishman delighted the audiences of the early and middle nineteenth century. Constance Rourke's delightful book, *American Humor*, gives eloquent testimony to this point. Then by the end of the nineteenth century and through the first thirty years of the twentieth, when vaudeville was in flower, the various circuits depended for their livelihood on a series of Dutch, Yiddish, Irish, and Negro dialect comedians. Even today their names still mean something. There were the blackface comedians like McIntyre and Heath who played the circuit from 1874 to 1930. No, neither one of those dates is a misprint; the dates and the span of time they represent merely seem incredible in this day and age when, we are told, a young comedian exhausts his entire repertoire in one season of television exposure. There was the great Irish team of Harrigan and Hart, which was so popular that it had its own theater. There was (and still occasionally is on television) the extremely volatile team of Smith and Dale, which could not even discuss the weather without getting into a violent argument. The team of Weber and Fields was most eclectic in its comedy. It played as Dutch, Yiddish, Irish, and blackface as the occasion demanded. I could go on and mention Gallagher and Shean, the delightful and lovable Bert Williams, who has frequently been described as the greatest of them all in vaudeville, and many, many others, but surely the point has been made.

Today we are obviously uneasy in the presence of dialect humor or dialect comedians even though there was a happy time when we were not. A few of the dialect comedians still survive, generally, although not exclusively, as night-club performers. Lou Holtz still tells his stories of Sam Lapides; Pat Harrington, Jr., under the patently absurd pseudonym of Guido Panzini, manages to get laughs from Italian dialect; Myron Cohen still appears with his Yiddish stories on the Ed Sullivan Show; Bill Dana transposes *j*'s and *h*'s when he plays the role of José Jiminez, a sad-eyed Mexican; but these are the exceptions. And in all the newspapers and in all the magazines, stories and articles constantly appear bemoaning the death of comedy. Comedy hasn't died; it has merely hibernated. And the long, cold winter will be over when we can once again listen to dialect humor with easy enjoyment.

That's why I was glad, despite my momentary uneasiness, to see *The Return of Hyman Kaplan*. It might turn out to be the first crocus of the spring that I have long been waiting for. That spring will surely arrive when the minority pressure groups no longer attempt to censor us out of our laughter. I resent censorship in any form, but I have some recourse when censorship is open and legalistic. I have practically none when a minority group tries to impose its desires on all the people by extra-legal means. If a minority group attempts censorship through the courts, then the opposition has a right to be heard. If the court decides in favor of the minority group, the opposition may be annoyed, but it no longer has grounds for resentment. But when the NAACP and the Anti-Defamation League of the B'nai B'rith and The Sons of Italy, organizations with which I am, most of the time, in sympathy, avoid the courts and bring pressure to bear upon a radio network, or a motion picture studio, or a television network, or a school system, or a publishing house, I have no recourse at all and my resentment runs high. And because of such organizations as the NAACP, the Anti-Defamation League, and The Sons of Italy (and I mention these three only as examples; there are many, many more) I have seen dialect humor decline.

Anything that is strong enough to survive should be strong enough to bear our laughter. If it can't, perhaps it shouldn't survive. None of the organizations mentioned seeks for complete assimilation of its members into the so-called "main stream of American Life," whatever that may be. Each seeks quite properly to preserve the cultural heritage of its group; each seeks quite properly to enhance its group's virtues, to minimize its group's failings; each quite properly takes pride in its group's individual and unique contributions to American life. Since all these things are true, it is strange that these organizations seemingly fail to realize that laughter is, after all, a social act. Despite the Freudian analysts, we laugh *with* far more than we laugh *at*. From dialect humor and the laughter which it produces we slowly arrive at an understanding of how the other fellow lives, how the other fellow thinks, what the other fellow's problems are. From understanding comes sympathy; and from sympathy and understanding working together comes empathy; and when these are accompanied by laughter, the understanding, the sympathy, and the empathy are not only painless but fruitful. We ought to have more Hyman Kaplans, more examples of dialect humor on the stage, on the screen, on radio, on television, in books and in magazines. And when we do, we shall have gone a long way in our attempt to liberate the comic spirit from at least one of the many nagging, querulous, artificial restraints.

We shall have gone a long way but not the whole way. After all, comedy has been under attack throughout recorded history. Twenty-five hundred years ago, Plato saw fit to attack Homer for representing the gods as giving vent to uncontrollable laughter at the sight of Hephaestus bustling from room to room. Six hundred years ago, Chaucer worried about his comic output and sought spiritual respectability in his "Retraction." One hundred years ago, Matthew Arnold employed his touchstone to determine that comic writers lacked high seriousness. And in recent years the Mort Sahls of the comic spectrum find themselves under attack when they poke fun at a President Eisenhower or a President Johnson. Perhaps the constant attacks have been instrumental in preserving comedy's vitality. Perhaps without them comedy would have become soft and flaccid, but I doubt it. Comedy will survive—as it has survived—with or without the attacks. Comedy's strength and integrity are not predicated on the influence of external forces for, at its best, comedy is as objective as a judge. It holds a mirror up to nature, to be sure, but its function is not merely reflective: comedy must and does make value judgments. It emphasizes reality, not illusion; truth, not falsehood; intellect, not emotion. Francisque Sarcey, the French theatrical critic of the late nineteenth century, admirably summarized this point in two lines of dialogue which he incorporated into a review:

COMEDIAN: That's how I feel the role.
SARCEY: Oh, that's too bad. Feeling isn't the question here, but understanding is.

Most comedians take "Uncle" Sarcey's advice quite literally. To them, understanding, not feeling, is the question at hand. Yet comedians are human beings with all the emotions and feelings of human beings. These emotions and feelings occasionally bring pressures to bear on the free action of the comic spirit. Friendliness toward an idea, an attitude, another human being may tend to cloud the comic vision. Most pressures the comedian is able to dispense with easily; the pressure of friendliness he finds hard to withstand. Yet he must withstand this ultimate pressure, for, in the last analysis, a comedian's only idea, only attitude, only friend must be truth. He can be a human being on his own time; when he is on public time —when he is writing or performing—nothing must be permitted to disturb the clear-eyed vision and the multi-faceted sanity which is comedy in action.

Bibliography

This bibliography is divided into three sections. The first section includes books, articles, novels, short stories, poems, plays, and musical comedies. The second section is devoted to motion pictures, and the third section to cartoons. Items in the first and third sections are listed alphabetically by authors and cartoonists; items in the second section are listed alphabetically by actors. Most often the actor or actress listed was the star of the film mentioned; on some occasions (the earliest

Chaplin films, for example), the actor listed was not the star, but his career is pertinent to the bibliography.

Section I

ABBOTT, GEORGE and DOUGLAS WALLOP. *Damn Yankees*. New York, 1956.

AGEE, JAMES. *Agee on Film*. New York, 1958.

ANONYMOUS. *Noah's Flood* and *The Second Shepherds' Play*, from *Specimens of the Pre-Shaksperean Drama*, ed. John Matthews Manly. 2 vols. Boston, 1897.

ANOUILH, JEAN. *La Petite Molière*. Paris, 1959.

APULEIUS. *The Golden Ass*, trans. W. Adlington. New York, 1935.

ARISTOPHANES. *The Comedies*, from *The Complete Greek Drama*, ed. Whitney J. Oates and Eugene O'Neill, Jr. 2 vols. New York, 1938.

ARISTOTLE. *The Poetics*, ed. and trans. I. Bywater. Oxford, 1909.

BARRY, PHILIP. *Holiday*, New York, 1929.

BEAUVOIR, SIMONE DE. *Must We Burn Sade?* New York, 1953.

BECKER, STEPHEN. *Comic Art in America*. New York, 1959.

BEHRMAN, S. N., adapter. *Amphitryon 38*, by Jean Giraudoux. New York, 1938.

BERGSON, HENRI. *Laughter*. New York, 1911.

BEVAN, DONALD and EDMUND TRZCINSKI. *Stalag 17*. New York, 1951.

BIERCE, AMBROSE. *The Devil's Dictionary*. New York, 1958.

BURNS, GEORGE, with CYNTHIA HOBART LINDSEY. *I Love Her, That's Why!* New York, 1955.

CAHN, WILLIAM. *The Laugh Makers*. New York, 1957.

CAIN, JAMES M. *Double Indemnity*. New York, 1943.

———. *Serenade*. New York, 1937.

CAPP, AL. "The Comedy of Charlie Chaplin," *The Atlantic*, CLXXXV, 2 (February, 1950), 25–29.

CHAUCER, GEOFFREY. *The Complete Works*, ed. W. W. Skeat. Oxford, 1920.

CLELAND, JOHN. *Memoirs of a Woman of Pleasure*. New York, 1963.

CLEMENS, SAMUEL L. (MARK TWAIN). *The Complete Humorous Sketches and Tales*, ed. Charles Neider. New York, 1961.

CLINTON-BADDELEY, V. C. *The Burlesque Tradition in the English Theatre after 1660*. London, 1952.

CONGREVE, WILLIAM. *Comedies*, ed. Bonamy Dobrée. London, 1951.

CONNELLY, MARC. *The Green Pastures*. New York, 1929.

COOPER, LANE. *An Aristotelian Theory of Comedy* [includes Cooper's translation of *Tractatus Coislinianus*]. New York, 1922.

CORNFORD, FRANCIS M. *The Origin of Attic Comedy*. London, 1914.

COWARD, NOEL. *Blithe Spirit*. New York, 1941.

CROCE, BENEDETTO. *Aesthetic*, trans. D. Ainslie. New York, 1955.

CROY, HOMER. "The Five Funniest Things in the World," *Photoplay*, XIV (September, 1918), 90–92.

DERVAL, PAUL. *The Folies Bergère*, trans. Lucienne Hill. London, 1955.

DRYDEN, JOHN. *The Dramatic Works*, ed. Montague Summers. 6 vols. London, 1931–1932.

EASTMAN, MAX. *Enjoyment of Laughter*. New York, 1936.

———. *The Sense of Humor*. New York, 1921.

FARNSWORTH, MARJORIE. *The Ziegfeld Follies*. London, 1956.

FAULKNER, WILLIAM. *Sanctuary*. New York, 1931.

FEIBLEMAN, JAMES. *In Praise of Comedy*. London, 1939.

FIELDING, HENRY. *Joseph Andrews*. London, 1910.

FOWLER, GENE. *Schnozzola*. New York, 1951.

FREUD, SIGMUND. *Wit and Its Relation to the Unconscious*, trans. A. A. Brill. New York, 1916.

FRYE, NORTHROP. *Anatomy of Criticism*. Princeton, 1957.

GIRAUDOUX, JEAN. *Amphitryon 38*. Paris, 1929.

GOODMAN, EZRA. *The Fifty-Year Decline and Fall of Hollywood*. New York, 1961.

GORDON, GEORGE. *Shakespearian Comedy*. Oxford, 1944.

GRACE, HARRY A. "Charlie Chaplin's Films and American Culture Patterns," *Journal of Aesthetics and Art Criticism*, X, 4 (June, 1952), 353–63.

GRIFFITH, RICHARD. *Marlene Dietrich, Image and Legend*. New York, 1959.

———and ARTHUR MAYER. *The Movies*. New York, 1957.

HAMMETT, DASHIELL. *The Maltese Falcon*. New York, 1930.

———. *Red Harvest*. New York, 1929.

———. *The Thin Man*. New York, 1934.

———. "The Girl with the Silver Eyes," from *Hammett Homicides*. New York, 1946.

———. "The Gutting of Couffignal," from *The Return of the Continental Op*. New York, 1945.

HAMMETT, DASHIELL. "Nightmare Town," from *Nightmare Town*. New York, 1948.

HASTINGS, WILLIAM T. "The Hardboiled Shakspere," *The Shakespeare Association Bulletin*, XVII (July, 1942), 114–25.

HEMINGWAY, ERNEST. *To Have and Have Not*. New York, 1937.

———. "The Killers," from *Men Without Women*. New York, 1927.

———. "A Man of the World," *The Atlantic*, CC, 5 (November, 1957), 64–66.

———. "The Short Happy Life of Francis Macomber," from *The Fifth Column, and the First Forty-Nine Stories*. New York, 1938.

HERRIMAN, GEORGE. *Krazy Kat* (with an Introduction by E. E. Cummings). New York, 1946.

HOBBES, THOMAS. *Human Nature*. Cambridge, 1928.

———. *Leviathan*. Oxford, 1946.

HOWARD, SIDNEY. *They Knew What They Wanted*. New York, 1925.

JONSON, BEN. *Five Plays*. London, 1953.

KANIN, GARSON. *Born Yesterday*. New York, 1946.

KAUFMAN, GEORGE S. and MORRIE RYSKIND. *Of Thee I Sing*. New York, 1932.

KEATON, BUSTER, with CHARLES SAMUELS. *My Wonderful World of Slapstick*. New York, 1960.

KNIGHT, ARTHUR. *The Liveliest Art*. New York, 1957.

KOESTLER, ARTHUR. *Insight and Outlook*. New York, 1949.

LANGER, SUSANNE K. *Feeling and Form*. New York, 1953.

LAURIE, JOE, JR. *Vaudeville: From the Honky-Tonks to the Palace*. New York, 1953.

LEE, GYPSY ROSE. *Gypsy, A Memoir*. New York, 1957.

LEONARD, HAROLD, ed. *The Film Index: A Bibliography*, vol. 1 [only one published]: *The Film as Art*. New York, 1941.

LERNER, ALAN JAY, and FREDERICK LOWE. *My Fair Lady*. New York, 1956.

LEWIS, C. S. *A Preface to "Paradise Lost."* London, 1942.

———. *The Screwtape Letters*. New York, 1944.

LOESSER, FRANK. *The Most Happy Fella*. New York, 1956.

LONGSTREET, STEPHEN. *High Button Shoes* [music by Jule Styne, lyrics by Sammy Cahn]. New York, 1949.

LUDOVICI, ANTHONY M. *The Secret of Laughter*. New York, 1933.

MACHIAVELLI, NICCOLÒ. *Mandragola*, trans. J. R. Hale. Oxford, 1956.

MANNES, MARYA. *More in Anger*. Philadelphia, 1958.

MARIE DE FRANCE. *Lais*, trans. Eugene Mason. London, n.d.

MARQUIS, DON. *archy and mehitabel*. New York, 1927.

MARTIAL. *The Epigrams*, trans. Walter C. A. Ker. 2 vols. London, 1947.

MARX, GROUCHO. *Groucho and Me*. New York, 1959.

MARX, HARPO, with ROWLAND BARBER. *Harpo Speaks*. New York, 1961.

MAUGHAM, W. SOMERSET. *Plays*. New York, 1935.

MEREDITH, GEORGE. *The Egoist*. New York, 1901.

———. *An Essay on Comedy*. New York, 1918.

MILTON, JOHN. *The Complete Poetical Works*, ed. Harris F. Fletcher. Boston, 1941.

NIKLAUS, THELMA. *Harlequin Phoenix*. London, 1956.

O'NEILL, EUGENE. *The Plays of Eugene O'Neill*. 3 vols. New York, n.d.

OVID. *The Art of Love*, trans. Rolfe Humphries. Bloomington, Indiana, 1957.

PETRONIUS. *Trimalchio's Dinner*, trans. Michael Heseltine. New York, 1939.

PLATO. *The Dialogues*, trans. B. Jowett. 3rd ed. 5 vols. London, 1892.

PLAUTUS. *The Amphitruo*, ed. Arthur Palmer. London, 1890.

———. *Plays*, trans. P. Nixon. 5 vols. Cambridge, Massachusetts, 1937.

POQUELIN, JEAN BAPTISTE (MOLIÈRE). *Théâtre Complet de Molière*, ed. Georges Monval. 8 vols. Paris, n.d.

———. *The Dramatic Works of Molière*, trans. Henri Van Laun. 6 vols. Edinburgh, 1876.

POST, EMILY (MRS. PRICE POST). *Etiquette*. New York, 1945.

POTTER, STEPHEN. *Sense of Humour*. New York, 1954.

RAMSAYE, TERRY. *A Million and One Nights*. New York, 1926.

ROSS, LEONARD Q. (LEO ROSTEN). *The Education of H*Y*-M*A*N K*A*P*L*A*N*. New York, 1937.

ROSTEN, LEO. *Hollywood: the Movie Colony, the Movie Makers*. New York, 1940.

———. *The Return of H*Y*M*A*N K*A*P*L*A*N*. New York, 1959.

ROURKE, CONSTANCE. *American Humor*. New York, 1931.

RUNYON, DAMON. "Sense of Humor," from *The Damon Runyon Omnibus*, New York, 1940.

SAYERS, DOROTHY L. *The Mind of the Maker*. London, 1941.

SELDES, GILBERT. *The Great Audience*. New York, 1950.

———. *The Public Arts*. New York, 1956.

Seldes, Gilbert. *The 7 Lively Arts*. Rev. ed. New York, 1957.

Shakespeare, William. *The Complete Works*, ed. George Lyman Kittredge. Boston, 1936.

Shaw, George Bernard. *Pygmalion*. Baltimore, 1956.

Sheridan, Richard Brinsley. *The Plays*. London, 1951.

Smith, H. Allen. *The Compleat Practical Joker*. New York, 1953.

Spewack, Samuel and Bella. *Kiss Me, Kate*. New York, 1953.

Stallings, Laurence, and Maxwell Anderson. *Three American Plays*. New York, 1926.

Swerling, Jo, Abe Burrows, and Frank Loesser. *Guys and Dolls*. New York, 1953.

Swift, Jonathan. "A Modest Proposal for Preventing the Children of Ireland from Being a Burden to Their Parents or Country," from *Satires and Personal Writings*, ed. William Alfred Eddy. New York and London, 1933.

Sypher, Wylie. "The Meanings of Comedy," from *Comedy*. New York, 1956.

Taylor, Robert Lewis. *W. C. Fields: His Follies and Fortunes*. New York, 1949.

Thackeray, William Makepeace. *English Humorists of the Eighteenth Century*. London, 1949.

Thurber, James. *The Years With Ross*. Boston, 1959.

———and E. B. White. *Is Sex Necessary?* New York, 1929.

Van Doren, Mark. *Shakespeare*. New York, 1947.

Van Druten, John. *The Voice of the Turtle*. New York, 1944.

West, Mae. *Goodness Had Nothing to Do With It*. Englewood Cliffs, New Jersey, 1959.

Wilde, Oscar. *The Plays*, intro. Edgar Saltus. New York, n.d.

Section II

Bara, Theda. *A Fool There Was* (1914).

Bogart, Humphrey, and Lauren Bacall. *To Have and Have Not* (1944).

Brynner, Yul, and Kay Kendall. *Once More With Feeling* (1960).

Cagney, James. *Public Enemy* (1931).

Chaplin, Charles. *The Adventurer* (1917).

———. *The Bank* (1915).

———. *Behind the Screen* (1916).

———. *By the Sea* (1915).

———. *Carmen* (1916).

CHAPLIN, CHARLES. *City Lights* (1931).
——. *The Count* (1917).
——. *The Cure* (1917).
——. *A Day's Pleasure* (1919).
——. *A Dog's Life* (1918).
——. *Easy Street* (1917).
——. *The Fireman* (1916).
——. *The Floorwalker* (1916).
——. *Getting Acquainted* (1914).
——. *The Gold Rush* (1925).
——. *The Great Dictator* (1940).
——. *His New Job* (1915).
——. *The Idle Class* (1921).
——. *The Immigrant* (1917).
——. *In the Park* (1915).
——. *A Jitney Elopement* (1915).
——. *The Kid* (1920).
——. *The Knockout* (1914).
——. *Making a Living* (1914).
——. *The Masquerader* (1914).
——. *Modern Times* (1936).
——. *Monsieur Verdoux* (1947).
——. *The New Janitor* (1914).
——. *A Night at the Show* (1915).
——. *One A.M.* (1916).
——. *The Pawnshop* (1916).
——. *The Pilgrim* (1923).
——. *Police* (1916).
——. *The Rink* (1916).
——. *The Rounders* (1914).
——. *Shanghaied* (1915).
——. *Shoulder Arms* (1918).
——. *Sunnyside* (1919).
——. *Tango Tangles* (1914).
——. *Tillie's Punctured Romance* (1914).
——. *The Tramp* (1915).
——. *Triple Trouble* (1915).
——. *The Vagabond* (1916).
——. *A Woman* (1915).
——. *Work* (1915).
CROSBY, BING, BOB HOPE, and DOROTHY LAMOUR. *Road to Morocco* (1942).
DAY, DORIS, and ROCK HUDSON. *Pillow Talk* (1959).

DIETRICH, MARLENE, and JAMES STEWART. *Destry Rides Again* (1939).
FIELDS, W. C. *The Bank Dick* (1940).
———. *The Barber Shop* (1933).
———. *The Fatal Glass of Beer* (1933).
———. *Million Dollar Legs* (1932).
———. *Never Give a Sucker an Even Break* (1941).
———. *The Pharmacist* (1932).
———. *Six of a Kind* (1934).
———and BING CROSBY. *Mississippi* (1935).
———and MAE WEST. *My Little Chickadee* (1940).
GABLE, CLARK and CLAUDETTE COLBERT. *It Happened One Night* (1934).
GRANT, CARY, and GRACE KELLY. *To Catch a Thief* (1955).
HEPBURN, KATHERINE, and CARY GRANT. *Bringing Up Baby* (1938).
HUTTON, BETTY. *Miracle of Morgan's Creek* (1944).
KEATON, BUSTER. *The Balloonatic* (1923).
———. *The Cameraman* (1928).
———. *Cops* (1922).
———. *The General* (1926).
———. *Go West* (1925).
———. *The Navigator* (1924).
———. *Our Hospitality* (1923).
———.*Sherlock, Jr.* (1924).
———and JAMES DURANTE. *What! No Beer?* (1933).
LANGDON, HARRY. *Boobs in the Woods* (1924).
———. *His Marriage Vow* (1924).
———. *Tramp, Tramp, Tramp* (1926).
LAUREL, STAN. *Mud and Sand* (1922).
LAUREL, STAN, and OLIVER HARDY. *Beau Hunks* (1931).
———. *Busy Bodies* (1932).
———. *Dirty Work* (1933).
———. *Pardon Us* (1931).
———. *Their First Mistake* (1932).
———. *Tit for Tat* (1935).
LEMMON, JACK, and SHIRLEY MACLAINE. *The Apartment* (1960).
LLOYD, HAROLD. *The Freshman* (1925).
———. *Grandma's Boy* (1922).
———. *High and Dizzy* (1920).
———. *I Do* (1921).
———. *Lonesome Luke on Tin Can Alley* (1917).
———. *Safety Last* (1923).

MARX BROTHERS. *Animal Crackers* (1930).
————. *The Big Store* (1941).
————. *Cocoanuts* (1929).
————. *A Day at the Races* (1937).
————. *Duck Soup* (1933).
————. *Horse Feathers* (1932).
————.*Monkey Business* (1931).
————. *A Night at the Opera* (1935).
————. *A Night in Casablanca* (1946).
MONROE, MARILYN. *The Seven Year Itch* (1955).
————and LAURENCE OLIVIER. *The Prince and the Showgirl* (1957).
————and TONY CURTIS. *Some Like It Hot* (1959).
MUNI, PAUL. *Scarface* (1932).
OLIVIER, LAURENCE. *King Henry V* (1944).
POWELL, WILLIAM, and MYRNA LOY. *The Thin Man* (1934).
ROBINSON, EDWARD G. *Little Caesar* (1930).
RUSSELL, JANE, and GILBERT ROLAND. *The French Line* (1954).
TURPIN, BEN. *The Shriek of Araby* (1923).
————and MADELINE HURLOCK. *Three and a Half Weeks* (1924).
WEST, MAE. *I'm No Angel* (1933).
————. *She Done Him Wrong* (1933).

Section III

BAKER, GEORGE. *Sad Sack*
BRICKMAN. *Blue Chips.*
CAPP, AL. *Li'l Abner.*
HERRIMAN, GEORGE. *Krazy Kat.*
JOHNSON, CROCKETT. *Barnaby.*
JOLITA. *Little Eve.*
KELLY, WALTER C. *Pogo.*
MCMANUS, GEORGE. *Bringing Up Father.*
MAULDIN, WILLIAM H. *Up Front.*
SCHULZ, CHARLES. *Peanuts.*
WILLARD, GEORGE. *Moon Mullins.*

Index

Abbott, George, *Damn Yankees*, 23, 26–29, 39–40
Absolute, Sir Anthony, 45–48, 50
Absolute, Captain Jack, 45–48, 50
Ace, Jane, 118
Adam, 48
Addams, Charles, 51, 67, 75
Adelaide, Miss, 108
Aeschylus, 40
Agathon, xi–xii
Agee, James, 89
Aguecheek, Sir Andrew, 34
Alceste, 78
Alcmena (Alkmena), 96, 99–103
Algernon, 105
Allen, Fred, 125
Allen, Gracie, 61, 64, 118
American Telephone and Telegraph Company, 124
Americans for Democratic Action, 113
Amos, 124
Amos 'n' Andy, 124
Amphitryon (Amphitruo) 95–97, 99–103
Amphitryon legend, 94
Amy, 91, 94
Anatol, 109
Anderson, Eddie, 125
Anderson, Maxwell, *What Price Glory?*, 52
Andy, 124
Anouilh, Jean, *La Petite Molière*, xi
Anti-Defamation League of B'nai B'rith, 127–28
Antony, 11, 42–43, 82
Apartment, The, 89
Applegate, Mr., 23, 26–29, 39–40
Apuleius, *The Golden Ass*, 69
Arabian Nights, The, 11, 78
Aristodemus, xii
Aristophanes, xii, xiii, 60, 68, 78; *The Birds*, 59; *The Clouds*, 45, 56
Aristotle, xii, xv, 40, 44, 64, 88; *The Poetics*, 39, 40
Armado, 50
Arnold, 106
Arnold, Matthew, xiii, 129

Asta, 88
Atlantic Monthly, 74
Audrey, 6
Augean stables, 99
Augustus, 60

Bacall, Lauren, 89
Baker's Wife, 90
Ballard, Kay, 118
Bara, Theda, 88; *A Fool There Was*, 88
Bardolph, 11
Barry, Philip, *Holiday*, 107
Beatrice, 15, 50
Beauvoir, Simone de, 71; *Must We Burn Sade?*, 71
Behrman, S.N., 95, 99; *Amphitryon 38*, 95, 99–103
Belch, Sir Toby, 6, 34–39
Belial, 27
Benedick, 15, 50
Benny, Jack, 117
Benvolio, 83
Bergerac, Cyrano de, 22
Bergson, Henri, xv, 12, 13, 19, 45, 49–50
Berman, Shelley, 115–17
Bertram, 24–25
Bevan, Donald, *Stalag 17*, 52
Bible, The, 122
Bilko, Sergeant Ernest, 54–55
Bishop, Joey, 115–17
Bob and Ray (Robert Goulding and Raymond Eliot), 119
Boccaccio, Giovanni, 73, 78
Bogart, Humphrey, 89; *To Have and Have Not*, 89
Bond, James, 75
Bottom, 62
Boyd, Joe, 27, 28
Bracken, Eddie, 89
Bradley, A.C., xii
Brecht, Bertolt, 79
Brickman, "Blue Chips," 119
Brock, Harry, 23, 29–33, 39–40
Bromia, 95
Brown, Miss Sarah, 108
Burns, George, 61, 64

Burrows, Abe, *Guys and Dolls*, 108–9
Buttons, Red, 22, 117

Caesar, Sid, 117
Cagney, James, 75; *Public Enemy*, 75
Cahn, Sammy, 47; "The Innocent Standerby," 47
Cain, James M., *Serenade*, 75; *Double Indemnity*, 75
Calhoun, Bill, 56
Caliban, 66
Callimaco, 92–94
Calvin and the Colonel, 124
Capp, Al, 51, 113, 125; *L'il Abner*, 51, 57, 125
Carmichael, Hoagy, 89
Carroll, Earl, 86
Carroll, Pat, 118
Cassidy, Ajax, 125
Cassio, 12
Cecily, 105
Célimène, 78
Cervantes Saavedra, Miguel de, 78
"Chad Gadya," 48–49
Channing, Carol, 79
Chaplin, Charles S., 4, 16, 22, 45, 47, 58, 62, 63; *By The Sea*, 47; *Carmen*, 47, 63; *City Lights*, 16, 62; *The Great Dictator*, 52, 63; *His New Job*, 47; *The Kid*, 59; *Modern Times*, 54; *Monsieur Verdoux*, 63; *A Night in the Show*, 47; *Shoulder Arms*, 52; *Tillie's Punctured Romance*, 88; *Triple Trouble*, 47; *Work*, 53
Chasuble, Canon, 105–6
Chaucer, Geoffrey, xiii, 69, 122; "Retraction," xiii, 129; *Troylus and Cryseyde*, 69
Chicago Sun-Times, 113
Cinna, 48
Claghorn, Senator, 125
Clark, Bobbie, 86
Clarke, Mae, 75
Cleland, John, *Fanny Hill or The Memoirs of a Woman of Pleasure*, 70
Clemens, Samuel L. (Mark Twain), *The Jumping Frog of Calaveras County*, 56
Cleopatra, 11, 42–44, 82
Cohen, Myron, 127
Colbert, Claudette, 88
Coleridge, Samuel Taylor, xii
Commedia dell'Arte, 78
Congreve, William, 78, 123; *The Way of the World*, 19, 78, 103–4, 109

Connelly, Marc, *Green Pastures*, 52
Cook, Joe, 118
Corio, Ann, 86
Cornford, Francis M., xv
Coward, Noel, *Blithe Spirit*, 109
Cranach, Lucas the Elder, 73
Crosby, Bing, 89; *The Road to Morocco*, 89
Cummings, E. E., 57–59
Curtis, Tony, 126

Dagmar, 83
Daiches, David, 77
Dali, Salvador, 75
Dana, Bill, 127
Dawn, Billie, 22, 30–33
Demarest, William, 89
Democratic party, 113
Detroit, Nathan, 108–9
Devery, 32
Dickens, Charles, 123; *David Copperfield*, 15–16
Dietrich, Marlene, 79, 88; *The Blue Angel*, 79; *Desire*, 79; *Destry Rides Again*, 88–89; *Morocco*, 79; *Shanghai Express*, 79
Diller, Phyllis, 118
Dodgson, Charles L. (Lewis Carroll), *Alice in Wonderland*, 73
Dogberry, 12, 14
Donald Duck, 56
Don John, 38
Doolittle, Alfred, 7–8, 16, 19
Dors, Diana, 83
Doyle, Sir Arthur Conan, 14
Dressler, Marie, 88; *Tillie's Punctured Romance*, 88
Dromio, 45
Dryden, John, *Amphitryon*, 95–99
Dumont, Margaret, 109
Dunne, Peter Finley, 112
Durante, Jimmy, 5, 56, 58–59, 117, 118–19
Dürer, Albrecht, 73

Eastman, Max, 23
"Easy Rider," 84
Eisenhower, Dwight D., 129
Elizabeth, 106
Ennius, 98
Eriximachus, xii
Eulenspiegel, Tyl, 79
Evans, Maurice, 38
Eve, 48

Fabian, 35, 37–38
Fag, 45–50
Falstaff, 5, 9, 11, 22, 62
Farmer in the Dell, The, 48

Faulkner, William, 73; *Sanctuary*, 73
Feibleman, James, *In Praise of Comedy*, 59
Feiffer, Jules, 113
Feste, 6, 8, 18, 22, 33–35, 37–39
Fielding, Henry, *Joseph Andrews*, 111
Fields, W. C., 16, 22, 56–57, 58, 59; *The Bank Dick*, 16, 59; *The Barber Shop*, 57; *My Little Chickadee*, 42
Fleming, Ian, 75
Fluellen, 11, 122
Fontanne, Lynn, 99
Fool (*King Lear*), 4
Fowler, Gene, *Schnozzola*, 5
France, Princess of, 56
Francis, 9, 10
"Frankie and Johnny," 84
French Line, The, 89
Freud, Sigmund, xv, 65, 67, 128

Gable, Clark, 88; *It Happened One Night*, 88
Gallagher and Shean, 126
Garbo, Greta, 89; *Ninotchka*, 89
Gilbert, Sir William Schwenck, *H.M.S. Pinafore*, 14; *The Mikado*, 14; *Pirates of Penzance*, 14
Giraudoux, Jean, 78; *Amphitryon 38*, 95, 99–103
Gleason, Jackie, 117
Glyn, Elinor, *Three Weeks*, 88
Gobel, George, 117
Goethe, Johann Wolfgang von, 78, 79
Goldberg, Jake, Mollie, Rosie, Sammy, 125
Goldoni, Carlo, 78
Goodman, Ezra, 51–52
Gordon, George, xii
Gordon, Helen, 74
Gower, 122
Graham, Fred, 56
Grant, Cary, 88; *Bringing Up Baby*, 88
Greenstreet, Sidney, 99
Gregory, Dick, 114
Gridiron Club, 52
Grimaldi, Joseph, 4
Grover, Sergeant Fred, 54–55
Gulliver, Lemuel, 112
Gwendolen, 105

Hall, Colonel John, 54
Hamlet, xiv, 18, 20
Hammer, Mike, 75
Hammett, Dashiell, 14, 75; "The Girl With the Silver Eyes," 75; "The Gutting of Couffignal," 75; *The Maltese Falcon*, 75; *Nightmare Town*, 75; *Red Harvest*, 75; *The Thin Man*, 75
Hardy, Oliver, 47
Harlequin, 4
Haroun-al-Raschid, 11
Harrigan and Hart, 126
Harrington, Pat Jr., 127
Hastings, William T., "The Hard-boiled Shakspere," 69–70
Hedges, Senator, 32
Heine, Heinrich, 78, 79
Helena, 24–25
Hemingway, Ernest, 73, 89; *To Have and Have Not*, 74, 89; "The Killers," 73–74; "A Man of the World," 74; "The Short Happy Life of Francis Macomber," 74
Henry IV (Bolingbroke), 9
Henry V (Hal), 9–11
Hepburn, Katherine, 88; *Bringing Up Baby*, 88
Hephaestus, xiii, 52, 128
Hercules, 97, 102
Herriman, George, 57–59; *Krazy Kat*, 57–59
Higgins, Mrs., 7–8
Higgins, Henry, 7–8
Hobbes, Thomas, xv
Hoffa, Portland, 118
Holmes, Sherlock, 14
Holtz, Lou, 125, 127
Homer, xiii, 78, 128
Hooper rating, 112
Hope, Bob, 89, 117; *The Road to Morocco*, 89
Hotspur, 9
House that Jack Built, The, 48
Howard, Sidney, 91; *They Knew What They Wanted*, 91–92, 94
Howard, Willie, 54
Hurlock, Madeline, *Three and a Half Weeks*, 88
Hutton, Betty, *The Miracle of Morgan's Creek*, 89

Iago, 12
Ignatz Mouse, 57–58
"I like a Man Who Takes His Time," 84
Illyria, 39
Ivy League, 67

Jack, 105
Jamy, 122
Jaques, 18, 80
Jocasta, 70
Joe, 91, 94
Joe the Joker, 56
John Birch Society, 113

Johnny, 107
Johnson, Lyndon B., 129
Johnson, Samuel, 89, 118
Jolita, *Little Eve*, 47, 56
Jones, Brutus, 18
Jonson, Ben, *Volpone*, 21, 62
Joseph, Saint, 95
Jourdain, Monsieur, 50
Julia, 107
Jupiter, 94–103

Kanin, Garson, *Born Yesterday*, 22, 23, 29–33, 39–40
Kaplan, Hyman, 121, 128
Kaufman, George S., *Of Thee I Sing*, 52
Kaye, Danny, 16–17
Keaton, Buster, 60, 63; *The General*, 52
Kelly, Walt, 113
Kemp, Will, 4
Keystone Comedies, 59
King, Alan, 115–17
Kingfish, 124
Kinsey reports, 112
Kitty, Lady, 106
Krazy Kat, 57–58
Kronenberger, Louis, 107

Lafew, 24–26
Lagado, Academy at, 112
Lamb, Charles, xii
Lamour, Dorothy, 89; *The Road to Morocco*, 89
La Rose, Rose, 86
Las Vegas, 86, 116
Laurel, Stan, 47, 88; *Mud and Sand*, 88
Lawd, 52
Lear, King, 4, 18
Leda, 101–2
Lee, Gypsy Rose, 86
Lee, Lorelei, 109
Lehrer, Tom, 63, 67
Lemmon, Jack, 126
Lerner, Alan Jay, *My Fair Lady*, 123
Levenson, Sam, 115–17
Lewis, C. S., 27; *The Screwtape Letters*, 29
Ligurio, 92
Lincoln, Abraham, 12
Linda, 107
Little Caesar, 75
Little Eve, 47
Loesser, Frank, 92; *Most Happy Fella*, 92; *Guys and Dolls*, 108
Lola, 27–28
Loman, Willy, 18

Longstreet, Stephen, *High Button Shoes*, 47
Loos, Anita, *Gentlemen Prefer Blondes*, 109
Lowe, Frederick, *My Fair Lady*, 123
Loy, Myrna, 88
Lucifer, 27
Lucrezia, 52, 92–94
Lunt, Alfred, 99
Luther, Martin, 29
Lyly, John, 103

Macbeth, 18
McCarthy, Senator Joseph, 113
Macduff, 48
Machiavelli, Niccolò, 78; *Mandragola*, 52, 55, 90, 92–94
McIntrye and Heath, 126
Mackenzie, Compton, 77
Macmorris, 122
Madam Queen, 124
Madison Avenue, 60, 67, 118
Mak, 45
Malaprop, Mrs., 19
Malvolio, 13, 23, 33–40, 53, 62
Mamie, 57
Mann, Sir Horace, 3
Mann, Thomas, *Felix Krull*, 79
Mannes, Marya, 87–88, 90; *More in Anger*, 87; "The Magic Box," 87–88, 90
Mansfield, Jayne, 83
Maria (*School for Scandal*), 105
Maria (*Twelfth Night*), 35–38
Mariana, 25
Marie de France, 78; *The Lais*, 69
Marlowe, Christopher, *Doctor Faustus*, 28
Marquis, Don, *archy and mehitabel*, 22
Martial, 69
Marx, Harpo, 8–9, 13–14, 45, 56
Marx Brothers, 8, 59, 109; *The Big Store*, 59; *A Day at the Races*, 8; *A Night at the Opera*, 53, 62; *A Night in Casablanca*, 13–14, 45
Masterson, Sky, 108
Matthew, Saint, 95
Maugham, W. Somerset, *The Circle*, 106
Mauldin, William H., 52, 113
Mencken, H. L., 86
Mercury, 94, 96–101
Mercutio, 15, 82–83
Meredith, George, 79; "An Essay on Comedy," xv, 78–79; *The Egoist*, 78
Micawber, Wilkins, 15–16
Middleton, Clara, 78

Middleton, Sally, 107
Millamant, 78, 103–4
Miller, Arthur, *Death of a Salesman*, 18
Milton, John, 67; *Paradise Lost*, 48
Minsky's, 85
Mirabell, 78, 103–4
Modern Theatre, 85
Monroe, Marilyn, 83
Moody, Titus, 125
More, St. Thomas, 29
Morgan, Henry, 119
Morgan, J. P., 52
Mosca, 21
Mother Goose, 73
Mrs. G. Goes to College, 125

Nagel, Conrad, 88
Nash, Paul, 51
National Association for the Advancement of Colored People, 127–28
National Distillers, 20
Naucrates, 98
Navarre, King of, 50, 56
Newhart, Bob, 115–17
New York Times, 51, 113
Nicia, Messer, 55, 92–94
Night, 98–99
Noah, 45, 57
Normand, Mabel, 45
Nussbaum, Mrs., 125

Octavius, 77
Oedipus, 18
Offissa Pupp, 57–58
Old Howard (Athenaeum), 85
Old Macdonald Had a Farm, 48
Olivia, 33–39
Olivier, Sir Lawrence, 122
Once More With Feeling, 89
O'Neill, Eugene, 91; *The Emperor Jones*, 18; *Desire Under the Elms*, 91
Orlando, 53, 55, 80–81
Orsino, 38–39
Ory, Kid, 89
Othello, 7, 18
Ovid, 78; *Metamorphoses*, 69; *Ars Amatoria*, 69

Page, Bill, 107
Pagliacci, 5, 18, 117
Pandarus, 69
Parolles, 23–27, 29, 38–40, 62
Partch, Virgil, 75
Patterne, Sir Willoughby, 78
Patucci, Tony, 91–92, 94
Paul, 30–33
Pavlov, Ivan Petrovich, 54

Pearl, Jack, 125
Perelman, S. J., 83, 120
Petronius, *Trimalchio's Dinner*, 69
Phaedrus, xii
Phidippides, 45
Philo, 82
Phogbound, Jack S., 125
Picasso, Pablo, 75
Pillow Talk, 89
Pious, Minerva, 125
Plato, xi–xiii, 11, 64, 128; *The Symposium*, xi–xii
Plautus, 78; *Amphitruo*, 45, 95–99
Polonius, 12
Pope, Alexander, *The Dunciad*, 70; "Epigram," 42
Popeye the Sailor, 63
Poquelin, Jean Baptiste (Molière), xiii, 78; *Amphitryon*, 95–99; *The Misanthrope*, 78; *The Would-Be Gentleman*, 50
Powell, William, 88; *The Thin Man*, 88
Prince and the Showgirl, 89
Pringle, Aileen, 88
Prism, Miss Laetitia, 21, 106
Prometheus, 72, 100

Rabelais, François, 73
Rand, C. H., 79
Reid, Ashton, 63
Republican party, 113
Reston, James, 113
Rich, John, 4
Richter, Jean Paul, 78, 79
Rise of the Goldbergs, 124–25
Ritzik, Sergeant Rupert, 54–55
Rogers, Will, 112, 113
Romeo, 83
Rosalind, 50, 53, 55, 80–82, 84
Rose, Carl, 51
Ross, Harold, 51
Rossillion, Countess of, 25
Rosten, Leo, *The Return of Hyman Kaplan*, 120–21, 123, 127
Rourke, Constance, *American Humor*, 61, 64, 126
Rumann, Sig, 45, 53, 62
Runyon, Damon, 108; "Sense of Humor," 56
Ryskind, Morrie, *Of Thee I Sing*, 52

Sacher-Masoch, Leopold von, 71–72
Sacks, Mike, 45, 86
Sade, Marquis de, 71–72
Sahl, Mort, 113, 129
St. Cyr, Lily, 86
St. Louis Post-Dispatch, 113
Sarcey, Francisque, 129

Satan, 48
Sayers, Dorothy, 14; *The Mind of the Maker*, 15
Sayonara, 22
Scarface, 75
Schnitzler, Arthur, *Anatol*, 109
Scotland Yard, 14
Sebastian, 38
Secunda Pastorum, 45, 95
Seldes, Gilbert, 57
Sennett, Mack, 47, 51–52
Seven Year Itch, 89
Shakespeare, William, 26, 69, 82, 90, 103, 122, 123; *All's Well That Ends Well*, 23–27, 29, 38–40, 62; *Antony and Cleopatra*, 42–44, 50, 64, 77, 82; *As You Like It*, 6, 18, 50, 53, 55, 80–82, 90, 106; *Comedy of Errors*, 45, 95, 103; *Hamlet*, 18, 20; *1 Henry IV*, 5–6, 9–12, 22, 62, 123; *2 Henry IV*, 11; *Henry V*, 10–12, 122–23; *Henry VI*, 69; *Julius Caesar*, 48; *King John*, 69; *King Lear*, 4, 18; *Love's Labour's Lost*, 50, 52, 56; *Macbeth*, 18, 48; *Measure for Measure*, 106; *Merchant of Venice*, 15; *Merry Wives of Windsor*, 123; *A Midsummer Night's Dream*, 62; *Much Ado About Nothing*, 15, 38, 50; *Othello*, 12, 18; *Richard III*, 69; *Romeo and Juliet*, 15, 82–83; *The Taming of the Shrew*, 123; *The Tempest*, 66; *Titus Andronicus*, 69; *Twelfth Night*, 6, 13, 18, 23, 33–40, 53, 54, 62, 106; *Venus and Adonis*, 69–70
Shaw, George Bernard, *Pygmalion*, 6–8, 16, 19, 123
Sheen, Bishop Fulton J., 112
Sheridan, Richard Brinsley, 123; *The Rivals*, 19, 45–50; *The School for Scandal*, 104–5
Shmoos, 51
Shrewsbury, Battle of, 9
Shylock, 15
Silvers, Phil, 54–55, 86
Skelton, Red, 117
Smith, H. Allen, 56
Smith and Dale, 126
Socrates, xi–xii
Some Like It Hot, 89, 126
Sons of Italy, 127–28
Sophocles, 40; *Oedipus Rex*, 18
Sosia, 45, 96–98
Sostrata, 52, 92–93
Sothern, Georgia, 86
Spade, Sam, 14
Spewack, Sam and Bella, *Kiss Me, Kate!*, 56

Spillane, Mickey, 75
Stallings, Laurence, *What Price Glory?*, 52
Sternberg, Josef von, 79
Stevens, Ashton, 86
Stewart, James, 88–89; *Destry Rides Again*, 88–89
Stravinsky, Igor, 75
Strepsiades, 45
Styne, Jule, "The Innocent Standerby," 47
Sullivan, Sir Arthur, *H.M.S. Pinafore*, 14; *The Mikado*, 14; *Pirates of Penzance*, 14
Sullivan, Ed, 127
Surface, Charles, 105
Swain, Mack, 45
Swerling, Jo, *Guys and Dolls*, 108
Swift, Jonathan, 4, 70, 73; *A Modest Proposal*, 63; *Gulliver's Travels*, 112
Swinburne, Algernon C., 73

Teazle, Lady, 104–5
Teazle, Sir Peter, 104–5
Teddie, 106
Thackeray, William Makepeace, 4, 123; *English Humourists of the Eighteenth Century*, 4
Thompson, Randall, 75
Thurber, James, 52; *Is Sex Necessary?*, 112; *The Years With Ross*, 51
Timoteo, Fra, 92–93
Tingler, The, 75
Tiresias, 95
To Catch a Thief, 89
Todd, Mike, *Around the World in Eighty Days*, 79
Tom and Jerry, 56
Touchstone, 6
Truman, Harry S., 15
Trzcinski, Edmund, *Stalag 17*, 52
Turpin, Ben, 88; *The Shriek of Araby*, 88; *Three and a Half Weeks*, 88

UNICEF, 17

Valentino, Rudolph, 88; *Blood and Sand*, 88; *The Sheik*, 88
Vanbrugh, Sir John, 70
Van Doren, Mark, 38
Van Druten, John, *The Voice of the Turtle*, 107
Van Gogh, Vincent, 68
Victoria Palace, 61
Vincentio, 11
Viola, 38, 54
Volstead, Andrew Joseph, 20

Wakefield *Noah*, 45, 57
Wallop, Douglass, *Damn Yankees*,
  23, 26–29, 39–40
Wall Street Journal, 119
Walpole, Horace, "Letter to Sir
  Horace Mann," 3
Ward, Artemus, 12
Washington Senators, 28
Weber and Fields, 126
West, Mae, 83–85, 86, 112; *She
  Done Him Wrong*, 83–84
White, E. B., *Is Sex Necessary?*, 112
Wilde, Oscar, 73, 105, 123; *The Im-
  portance of Being Earnest*, 21, 55,
  105–6

Willard, George, *Moon Mullins*, 57
Williams, Bert, 126
Williams, Michael, 10–11
Willie, 57
Wilson, Marie, 83
Wimsey, Lord Peter, 14
Wishfort, Lady, 19, 109
Would-Be, Sir Politic, 62
Wycherley, William, 70; *The Coun-
  try Wife*, 90
Wynn, Ed, 22

Ziegfield, Florenz, 86, 107